CONTACT USA 2

READING AND VOCABULARY

Paul Abraham
Daphne Mackey

Longman

longman.com

Contact USA 2: Reading and Vocabulary

Pearson Education, 10 Bank Street, White Plains, NY 10606

Executive editor: Sherry Preiss
Senior acquisitions editor: Laura Le Dréan
Development editor: Stacey Hunter
Vice president, director of design and production: Rhea Banker
Executive managing editor: Linda Moser
Senior production manager: Raymond Keating
Associate production editor: Christopher Leonowicz
Senior manufacturing buyer: Nancy Flaggman
Cover and interior design: Ann France
Text composition: TSI Graphics
Text font: 12/13.5 Minion
Text art: Bradley Clark

ISBN: 0-13-049625-1

LONGMAN ON THE **WEB**

Longman.com offers online resources for teachers and students. Access our Companion Websites, our online catalog, and our local offices around the world.

Visit us at **longman.com.**

Printed in the United States of America

1 2 3 4 5 6 7 8 9 10- PBT -07 06 05 04 03

Contents

To the Teacher

Contact USA 2: Reading and Vocabulary is a text for low-intermediate students of English. Although its structure and exercises are aimed primarily at developing academic reading skills and vocabulary, its content is appropriate for all non-native English speakers. The readings provide background information about topics of interest in American culture. The topics were chosen to engage students in both the reading task and subsequent class discussions. The variety of reading types gives students practice with charts, graphs, and first, and third-person narratives. The exercises and discussion questions build students' vocabulary while allowing them to respond to the ideas presented in the text.

Reading

Most students at this level are able to read and understand more in English than they are able to produce. Therefore, the readings may be challenging for students at this level, but the exercises require lower-level reading and vocabulary skills. Students work on the essential reading skills of identifying main ideas and details, scanning, skimming, reading charts and graphs, reading for speed, and making inferences.

The first reading in every chapter is a general overview that introduces key vocabulary related to the subject. Reading for Specific Information (Look Again) and the Timed Reading (A Point of View) provide new perspectives on the subject and closely tie in with the speaking activities in each chapter. Students are encouraged to express their ideas about the subject. Since these readings are often based on opinions and are, as such, debatable, we encourage you to contribute your own personal points of view and to express your own cultural perspectives in any way that might expand your students' knowledge or spark their interests.

Vocabulary

The vocabulary focus moves from understanding general meaning within the context of the readings to active use of new words in speaking and writing. The recycling of key vocabulary items throughout the book promotes successful acquisition. Students learn approximately 300 new words, phrases, and expressions in the contexts of the main reading and two shorter readings. An important feature of *Contact USA 2* is the amount of practice students get with new vocabulary. Each chapter offers at least nine different vocabulary exercises, including guessing meaning from context, multiple-choice, editing, cloze, and matching.

The meaning of much of the vocabulary is implied within the readings, and the vocabulary exercises encourage students to guess meaning from context. To help build this essential reading skill we discourage the use of dictionaries.

Chapter Outline

A First Look

A.   Background Building
B.   Reading
C.   Topic
D.   Scanning/Vocabulary
E.   Reading Comprehension

Look Again

A.   Vocabulary
B.   Reading Comprehension
C.   Reading for Specific Information
D.   Think About It

A Point of View

A.   Background Building
B.   Timed Reading
C.   Vocabulary
D.   React

Vocabulary Review

A.   (Using expressions)
B.   (Using vocabulary)
C.   (Matching vocabulary)

The **Teacher's Manual** contains Teaching Guidelines, Teaching Suggestions by Chapter, the student book answer key, Vocabulary Review Tests for each chapter, their answer keys, and three additional Reading Tests.

To the Student

Welcome to *Contact USA 2: Reading and Vocabulary.* This book has two goals: to improve your reading ability, and to improve your vocabulary.

Working with others and learning from each other is an important part of improving your reading skills and your general English language ability. While studying with this book, you will have many opportunities to work with other students in pairs and in small groups. We hope that together you will enjoy reading, writing, and talking about interesting topics in American culture.

Acknowledgments

Our thanks to the editors at Pearson Longman ELT who have encouraged us to write these lower-level readers for many years, to Laura Le Dréan, who finally made it happen, and to Stacey Hunter, who did an outstanding job as development editor. We would also like to thank the reviewers of the manuscript:

Linda Boice, Elk Grove Adult Education, Sacramento, CA; **Abigail Brown**, TransPacifc Hawaii College, Honolulu, Hawaii; **David Dahnke**, North Harris College, Houston, TX; **Dixie Fitzgerald**, Hialeah Senior High School, Hialeah, FL; **Sara McKinnon**, College of Marin, Kentfield, CA; **Laura Shier**, Portland State University, Portland, OR; **Christa Snow**, Nationalities Service Center, Philadelphia, PA; **Safineh Tahmassebi**, University of California, Irvine, CA; **Murat Yesil**, former ESL teacher, Istanbul, Turkey.

Paul Abraham
Daphne Mackey

Chapter 1 Friends

A FIRST LOOK

A BACKGROUND BUILDING

Make a list of the names of your friends below. Then discuss the questions in small groups.

My Friends	

1. Are some people you listed closer or more important friends than others?

2. Where did you meet these friends? At school or work? Did you grow up together or meet while you were doing the same activities?

3. Do you have a "best" friend? Do you have a lot of friends or just a few good ones?

Friendship

1   *When I'm in trouble, I can always call him for help. If I have a problem, just talking to her makes me feel better.* These are some things people might say about friends. Friends are the people who know you, understand you, and accept you as you are. Friends, unlike family, choose each other and decide to be 5 connected. While family are the people who have to take you in, friends are the people who choose to take you in.

2   What is a friend? Friendship is a relationship between two people. It is voluntary and mutual. Voluntary means that people choose to be friends. Mutual means that friendship is two-   10 sided and equal. Although relatives may be friends, friends are not related by blood. They are usually not brothers, sisters, or cousins.

3   How do people become friends? Friends usually have some common experiences. They went to the same school,   15 grew up in the same town, or they work in the same company, or live in the same neighborhood. Friends may also enjoy the same activities. They might play softball together, belong to the same health club, or see each other at their children's soccer games. Friends also meet through other friends.   20

4   There seem to be different kinds of friends as well. There are those who have been friends for many years and know each other's life stories. There are friends who talk and share their deepest feelings with each other, and there are friends who do things together. They bicycle, play cards, or go out   25 to dinner.

5   Friendship is also different in different cultures. In some cultures, responsibility to friends is very important. Close friends drop everything to help each other because friendships are highly valued, a top priority. In other cultures, people are   30
too busy with work and family to have close friendships. They are satisfied with casual friendships. They don't feel the need to have very close relationships.

6   Friends may become even more important in the future. More people are moving away from their families. Families are   35
becoming smaller. Some people are choosing not to get married or are waiting longer to get married. For some people, friends may become a new type of family. Friends are an important part of life. They bring us companionship, connection to others, and good times. Friends take time and energy, but   40
they are worth it.

C ▶ TOPIC

Each paragraph in the reading has one main idea, its topic. Read the topics below. Match each topic to a paragraph in the reading. Write the number of the paragraph on the line.

___4___   different types of friends

_____   the importance of friends in the future

_____   ways that people become friends

_____   cultural differences in friendships

_____   examples of the importance of friends

_____   a definition of friendship

D SCANNING/VOCABULARY

Part 1

It is important to be able to find information quickly when you read. This is called scanning. Scan the reading for the word in column A. Write the number of the line where you find the word. Then compare the word in column A to the word(s) in column B. Are the meanings similar or different? Write **S** (similar) or **D** (different) on the line.

	A	Line Number	B	S or D?
1.	voluntary	9	not by choice	D
2.	mutual		one-sided	
3.	related		of the same family	
4.	common		different	
5.	belong to		be part of	
6.	deepest		strongest	
7.	responsibility		something you have to do	
8.	priority		something that is not important	
9.	satisfied		unhappy	
10.	casual		very close	
11.	companionship		friendship	
12.	worth it		not valuable	

Part 2

Complete the sentences with the words from the box.

accept	choose	~~connected~~	responsibility	voluntary
belong to	common	priority	satisfied	worth

1. Most people want to feel __connected__ to other people, like their family and friends.

2. I take _____ for the accident. I'll pay to repair the car.

3. You can do it, but you don't have to. It's _____.

4. Are you _____ with your work, or are you looking for another job?

5. Friends often have _____ experiences. For example, their children might play on the same sports team.

6. They think about saving money all the time. It's their number one _____.

7. They _____ a church in their neighborhood.

8. You should _____ her for your team. She plays soccer very well.

9. I try to _____ people as they are. I don't try to make them change.

10. Studying hard in school is _____ your time because it can help you in the future.

E ▸ READING COMPREHENSION

Circle the letter of the word or phrase that best completes each sentence.

1. Friends are _____ families because friends choose each other and family members do not.
   a. similar to
   b. not like
   c. the same as

2. People in your family have to accept you, but your friends _____ to accept you.
   a. have
   b. know how
   c. decide

3. According to the first paragraph, people say that when they have difficulty, they call a friend for help or just to _____ a friend.
   a. look for
   b. talk to
   c. understand

4. Friendship is voluntary and _____.
   a. related
   b. equal
   c. casual

5. _____ are not usually related by blood.
   a. Brothers
   b. Cousins
   c. Friends

6. People are friends because they have some common experiences, enjoy _____ activities, or because they have met through other friends.
   a. each other
   b. the same
   c. different

7. The reading discusses _____ types of friends.
   a. two
   b. three
   c. many

8. _____ friends probably wouldn't drop everything to help each other.
   a. Casual
   b. Highly valued
   c. Close

9. The reading says that in the future friends _____.
   a. may get married
   b. may choose not to get married
   c. may be like family

10. The author thinks that friends take _____, but they are worth it.
    a. good times
    b. energy
    c. companionship

LOOK AGAIN

A ▶ VOCABULARY

Circle the letter of the word that best completes each sentence.

1. You don't have to give money to that group. Giving is completely _____.
   a. equal   **b.** valued   **c.** voluntary

2. Good grades are my top _____. I want to do well in school.
   a. priority   **b.** worth   **c.** connection

3. I had a terrible _____ yesterday while I was shopping. When I opened my wallet to pay, I realized that I didn't have enough money.
   a. responsibility   **b.** experience   **c.** relationship

4. He is the teacher. It's his _____ to take care of class activities.
   a. expression   **b.** leisure   **c.** responsibility

5. You have to _____ your in-laws. They're your family.
   a. choose   **b.** accept   **c.** decide

6. They are good friends. He helps her and she helps him. It's a _____ relationship.
   a. mutual   **b.** natural   **c.** regular

7. Are you _____ to her? The two of you look a lot alike.
   a. connected   **b.** related   **c.** identified

8. Are you _____ with this school, or are you planning to go to a different one?
   a. satisfied   **b.** equal   **c.** casual

9. I _____ a health club, but I almost never have time to go.
   a. decide   **b.** manage   **c.** belong to

10. They are _____ friends. They don't see each other very often.
    a. casual   **b.** regular   **c.** mutual

B READING COMPREHENSION

Use the words below to complete a summary of the reading.

activities	cultures	~~friends~~	times	valued
choose	experiences	mutual	together	voluntary
connection	family	talk	unlike	

Friends choose each other. They decide to be _____friends_____.

1

Friends are _____ family because people don't

2

_____ their families; friendship is _____. It

3   4

is also usually _____, or two-sided.

5

People often become friends because they share some common

_____ or enjoy the same _____.

6   7

There are different types of friends. There are those who have known

each other for many years, those who like to _____ to each

8

other and share their feelings, and those who like to do things

_____.

9

Friendship is different in different _____.

10

Responsibility to friends is highly _____ in some cultures.

11

In others, it is not as important.

In the future, friends may become a new type of _____.

12

Having friends is not easy, but friendship brings us good

_____ and _____ to others.

13   14

C READING FOR SPECIFIC INFORMATION

Read the following passage about a person's early experience with making friends in the United States and discuss the questions that follow with a partner.

> When I first learned English, I was very confused about what people were saying. "Let's get together." "See you later." "I'll give you a call." We never got together or saw each other later, and they never gave me a call. I finally realized that these are just friendly expressions, not really invitations. Now I understand the difference, and my first contact with new people is much easier.

1. What was the problem for this person?

2. What changed?

3. Have you ever had a similar experience?

D THINK ABOUT IT

Discuss the questions in a small group.

1. Do you think that relatives can also be friends?

2. If you had a problem with your car late at night, who would you call for help, a relative or a friend?

3. How does the writer feel about meeting people now?

A BACKGROUND BUILDING

Discuss these questions about the picture.

1. Where are these people?

2. What are they doing?

3. How do they feel?

Read the passage. Then read the sentences on page 14. Write T (true), F (false), or ? (not sure). You have four minutes.

I've made a lot of friends since I first came to the university in the United States, but I still don't understand friendships here that well. There is a guy, Rick, who lives across the hall in my dormitory. We took some classes together last semester and got to know each other. We play soccer on the school team and go to a lot of the same parties. We eat together a lot at the cafeteria. I guess you could say that we're friends.

Well, a few weeks ago, my brother came for a visit. I decided to invite a few of the guys from the dorm out to dinner downtown to meet my brother and to have a good meal. When I invited Rick, he said "sure" and I told him to meet us at the restaurant at 8:00.

Everyone but Rick had arrived by 8:00 so we waited for him. When he didn't show up by 8:30, I gave him a call. He answered the phone and said that "something had come up." I went back to the table and we ordered dinner.

The next afternoon, I saw Rick and he said that he was sorry that he couldn't make it to the dinner and that he would meet my brother another time. I told him that my brother had already gone home. He said that was too bad and that he would see me later.

I haven't seen much of Rick since then and I don't understand what happened. I thought that we were friends, but I guess that I made a mistake.

_____?_____ 1. The writer has many friends back home.

_____ 2. Rick and the writer are old friends.

_____ 3. Rick and the writer are roommates.

_____ 4. Rick and the writer go to the same school.

_____ 5. The writer has other friends.

_____ 6. The writer's brother was visiting.

_____ 7. Rick showed up for the dinner.

_____ 8. Rick couldn't come to the dinner because something important happened.

_____ 9. The writer is still a casual friend of Rick's.

_____ 10. The writer thought that he and Rick were friends.

C VOCABULARY

Circle the letter of the word or phrase closest to the meaning of the boldfaced word(s).

1. He **came to** the party at 9:30.
   a. arrived at   b. attended   c. left

2. I **got to know them well** last summer.
   a. met them one time   b. spent a lot of time with them   c. talked about them

3. She **gave me a call** at 3:00 last night.
   a. telephoned me   b. shouted to me   c. called my name

4. I **realized** that we were not friends.
   a. guessed   b. thought   c. learned

5. They always **show up** late for morning classes.

    a. take off   **b.** arrive   **c.** get up

6. They couldn't **make it to** the reception because their son was sick.

    a. do   **b.** know about   **c.** be at

7. Let's **order** coffee.

    a. ask for   **b.** make   **c.** take

8. Something **came up** and I couldn't call you.

    a. happened   **b.** arrived   **c.** showed

9. Some **guys** from my hometown came to visit.

    a. ancestors   **b.** men   **c.** children

10. I **guess** that I made a mistake.

    a. understand   **b.** know   **c.** think

D REACT

1. Work in a small group. Discuss this question: What do you think happened between the two "friends" in the reading?

2. Work with a partner. Read the following sayings and talk about their meanings. Which one is the most interesting to you?

> - *Friends are like flowers in the garden of life.*
>
> - *Make new friends, but keep the old, since one is silver, and the other gold.*
>
> - *You never know how many friends you have until you have a house at the beach.*

VOCABULARY REVIEW

A In English, words often go together to form expressions. For example, we often say *grow up*, as in He *grew up* in New York. When you read, look for expressions. Here are words from this chapter that form expressions.

VERBS	OTHER EXPRESSIONS
belong to	confused about
get together (with someone)	in trouble
get to know (someone)	satisfied with
grow up	
make friends	
share with	
show up	

Part 1

Complete the sentences with expressions from the box.

1. I don't understand our math homework. I'm __confused about__ the problems we have to do.

2. Did you forget to bring your lunch? I have a big lunch here and I'll _____ you.

3. My sister came home very late last night and my parents are angry. She's _____.

4. Did you _____ here in the city, or are you from somewhere else?

5. I _____ a gym downtown, so I go there a lot.

6. I'm _____ this class. I'm learning a lot.

7. Let's _____ this weekend. Maybe we can go to the movies.

8. They never _____ on time. They're always late.

9. Sometimes it's hard to _____ when you move to a new place by yourself.

10. My neighbors seemed very nice, but I didn't _____ them very well. They moved after only two months.

Part 2

The following sentences are not correct. Add the words from the box to the sentences to make them correct. There may be more than one possible answer.

about	in	together	with
for	to	~~up~~	

1. Be on time. Don't show ^up^ late.

2. When you live with roommates, you really get know them.

3. Let's wait everyone to arrive before we start eating.

4. Do you belong this club?

5. Where did she grow?

6. I get with my brothers once a month.

7. He's not studying. His grades are bad. He's trouble.

8. Alice forgot her book. Can you share yours her?

9. I am really confused my schedule for next week.

10. He is going to change schools. He's not satisfied this one.

Part 3

Use the expressions from the list on page 16 to complete the questions. Then ask a classmate the questions. Part of the expression may already be in the sentence.

1. How often do you and your good friends _get together_ ?

2. When you were _____ing _____, did you have many close friends?

3. If you were _____, who would you call for help?

4. Imagine that you just moved to a new city. What do you think is the best way to _____?

B Complete the sentences with words from the box.

belong	common	connection	relationship	voluntary
casual	companionship	related	satisfied	worth

1. You don't have to go into the army in my country. It is

   _____.

2. John and Kim have a very good _____. They really care
   for each other.

3. Everyone thinks that my friend, John, and I are brothers, but we aren't
   _____ at all.

4. I _____ to a book club. We meet once a month to talk
   about a book we have all read.

5. How does your family know her family? What's the _____?
   Are you neighbors?

6. I have lunch with Anne once in a while and we talk about work. We're
   not very close. We're _____ friends.

7. Robert spends every weekend studying. It's _____ it to
   him because he wants to go to a good university.

8. Things are going well in my life. I have a good job without much stress.
   I'm _____.

9. _____ is very important in marriage.

10. Jan and Bill became friends because they had a _____
    interest in art.

C Match each word or phrase to the word or phrase with a similar meaning.

__g__	1. unlike	**a.**	duty
_____	2. voluntary	**b.**	happy `
_____	3. common	**c.**	most important thing
_____	4. responsibility	**d.**	companionship
_____	5. friendship	**e.**	shared
_____	6. choose	**f.**	connected
_____	7. related	**g.**	not similar to
_____	8. satisfied	**h.**	be part of
_____	9. priority	**i.**	by your own choice
_____	10. belong to	**j.**	select

1. <u>   forest   </u>

2. _____

3. _____

4. _____

5. _____

6. _____

beach	~~forest~~	lake
desert	grassy lawn	mountains

A FIRST LOOK

A BACKGROUND BUILDING

1. Look at the pictures and words on page 22. Match the name of the place with its picture. Use the words in the box.

2. Close your eyes for one minute. Imagine that you are in a place where you feel happy and relaxed. Now answer the questions.

   a. Were you alone or with other people?

   _____

   b. Were you inside a building, or outside?

   _____

   c. What are three things that you saw in this place?

   _____

3. Work with a partner. Describe your "place" to your partner.

4. Work with the whole class and complete the chart. Count how many classmates imagined each place described in the chart. Write the number in the chart. Then discuss your results.

Place Description	Class Total
Inside	
Outside	
In the city	
In the country	
In the mountains	
At the beach	
Near a lake	
On a grassy lawn	
Other	

What's in a Place?

1   What's in a place? By this question we want to ask, what meanings do places or locations have? They have many meanings. A place can mean silence or noise, safety or excitement.

2   When they are asked to think of a favorite location, many 5 people mention home. "There's no place like home" is an old expression. It means that no other place is as good as a person's home.

3   Many people have favorite places at home. Some prefer the kitchen; some like their bedrooms and others like to be 10 outside in the yard. We know that many Americans watch a lot of television each week. Maybe the favorite place for most Americans is where the TV is.

4   Psychologist Roger Ulrich asked people from all over the world which outside locations they preferred. He found that 15 people prefer open landscapes of hills, small groups of trees, and grassy lawns. Even people who grew up in forests, deserts, in the mountains, or on the coast prefer this kind of scenery. Why? It seems to relate to man's history on the savannas of Africa. Savannas are open, grassy lands. In the 20 past, people were able to find food there, and there were few animals that could hurt them.

5   Place can mean more than location, however. It can show the importance of a person's position in a company. For example, the location of a person's desk in the office can 25

show his or her place or position in a company. Where is the manager's desk? Is it in a large office with windows? Where does the most important person sit at the meeting? Is it at the head of the table?

6   *Place* is a simple word, but it has a lot of very different meanings.   30

C ▸ TOPIC

Read the topics below. Match each topic to a paragraph in the reading. Write the number of the paragraph on the line.

_____ home as a favorite place

_____ studies of favorite places outside

_____ favorite places at home

_____ the word *place* has many meanings

_____ place can show importance of a person's job

_____ the meaning of the title

D SCANNING/VOCABULARY

Part 1

Scan the reading for the word in column A. Write the number of the line where you find the word. Then compare the word in column A to the word(s) in column B. Are the meanings similar or different? Write **S** (similar) or **D** (different) on the line.

A	Line Number	B	S or D?
1. place		location	
2. silence		noise	
3. excitement		safety	
4. mention		say	
5. home		place to live	
6. expression		group of words	
7. prefer		dislike	
8. outside		inside	
9. scenery		landscape	
10. history		past	
11. position		job	
12. head		top person or part of something	

Part 2

Complete the sentences with words from the box.

excitement	history	noise	place	prefer
head	mention	outside	position	scenery

1. When I take the train, I look out the window to see the beautiful _____.

2. I need a quiet _____ where I can study.

3. What do you _____ doing on your vacation, going to the beach or to the mountains?

4. The young girl was filled with _____ when she got to the amusement park.

5. That's not music to me. It sounds like _____.

6. It's rainy and windy _____. Let's stay in and watch a movie on television.

7. On his birthday, the little boy was very excited to sit at the _____ of the table.

8. What is your _____ at the company? Are you a manager?

9. People often _____ home when you ask them what their favorite place is.

10. I'm studying _____. I'm very interested in learning about the past.

Circle the letter of the word or phrase that best completes each sentence.

1. According to the author, a place has _____ meanings.

    a. no **b.** many **c.** some

2. Some people prefer _____ places like the yard.

    a. outside **b.** inside **c.** beside

3. The author thinks that the favorite inside place of many Americans is _____.

    a. in the kitchen **b.** in front of the **c.** in the backyard
    television

4. Ulrich asked people what kind of _____ they liked best.

    a. landscapes **b.** buildings **c.** savannas

5. People _____ forests, deserts, mountains, or coasts.

    a. remembered **b.** liked **c.** did not prefer

6. A savanna is a type of _____.

    a. country **b.** small tree **c.** landscape

7. People may prefer savannas because of _____ in Africa.

    a. the need for food **b.** the animals **c.** man's history

8. Location within an office can show the importance of a person's position or _____.

    a. safety **b.** job **c.** boss

9. The person who sits at the head of the table at a meeting is probably _____.

    a. a young worker **b.** an assistant **c.** a manager

10. According to the reading, place means _____.

    a. many different **b.** simple things **c.** silence or noise
    things

LOOK AGAIN

A VOCABULARY

Circle the letter of the word or phrase that best completes each sentence.

1. Mary is not in the house. She's _____.
   - **a.** in place
   - **b.** inside
   - **c.** outside

2. What's your _____ weekend activity?
   - **a.** open
   - **b.** favorite
   - **c.** natural

3. Do you know the _____ of this word?
   - **a.** place
   - **b.** question
   - **c.** meaning

4. The middle of a big city is usually a place with a lot of _____.
   - **a.** safety
   - **b.** noise
   - **c.** silence

5. A _____ is a type of landscape.
   - **a.** desert
   - **b.** store
   - **c.** world

6. Which do you _____, skiing or swimming?
   - **a.** dislike
   - **b.** prefer
   - **c.** mention

7. There is not much water in a _____.
   - **a.** lake
   - **b.** desert
   - **c.** location

8. The head of a group of workers is the _____.
   - **a.** oldest
   - **b.** manager
   - **c.** location

9. What are you trying to _____ in this picture?
   - **a.** hold
   - **b.** show
   - **c.** prefer

10. They need to talk about the problem in their next _____.
   - **a.** meaning
   - **b.** meeting
   - **c.** location

B ▸ READING COMPREHENSION

Find the answers to the questions in the reading. Underline the answers in the reading and write the number of the question next to its answer.

1. According to the reading, when people are asked about their favorite place, what do many people say?

2. Why do the authors mention television?

3. What are two types of outside places the reading mentions?

4. What did Ulrich find out?

5. Why do people prefer this type of landscape?

6. How is the importance of a person's position in a company sometimes shown?

C ▸ READING FOR SPECIFIC INFORMATION

Read the passage. Then complete the diagram on page 31 with information from the passage.

Place has meaning for all people, but it had a special importance in ancient China. There, nearly 4,000 years ago, farmers recognized the importance of how things are placed. For example, they recognized that the best place to put a garden is on the south side of a house. Why? Because the north side is colder and has less sun.

The placement of things became the art of Feng Shui (pronounced fung shway). Today this art of placement has become very popular throughout the world, including in the United States. In Feng Shui, each part of a person's home represents an area of his or her life. For example, the entrance door represents a person's career and it faces north. The south side of a house represents fame. Fame means being known and admired by many people. The east represents family and the past, and the west, children and new ideas.

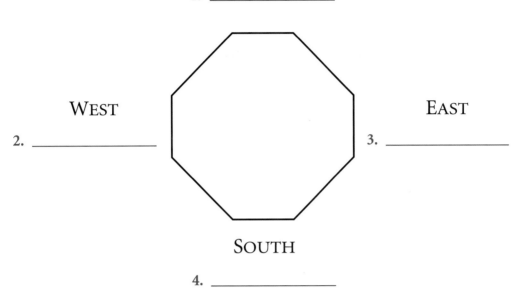

NORTH

1. _____career_____

WEST

2. _____

EAST

3. _____

SOUTH

4. _____

D ▸ THINK ABOUT IT

1. Feng Shui philosophy gives some very practical ideas. Read the ideas below. Check (✓) the ones that you agree with.

_____ Keep your rooms clean.

_____ Put things away, in their place.

_____ Don't have a television or a computer in your bedroom.

_____ Have your desk face the door.

_____ Don't have a lot of furniture in the living room.

2. Work with a partner. Explain why you agree or disagree with each statement in #1.

House Plan 1

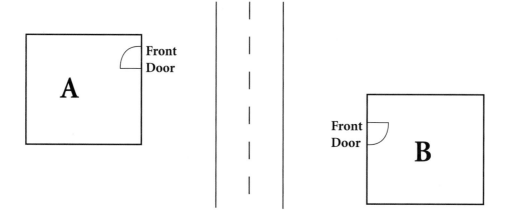

House Plan 2

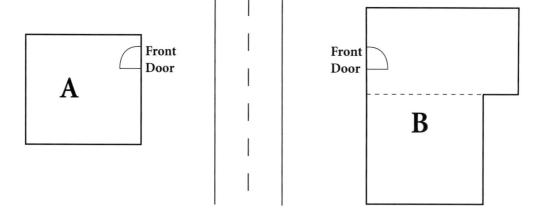

A BACKGROUND BUILDING

Look at the figures on page 32. Check (✓) the statements that are true.

House Plan 1

_____ 1. The houses are next to each other.

_____ 2. House A is smaller than House B.

_____ 3. The houses are across the street from each other.

_____ 4. The doors face each other.

House Plan 2

_____ 1. The houses face each other.

_____ 2. The houses are across the street from each other.

_____ 3. The doors face each other.

_____ 4. House A is smaller than House B.

Read the passage. Then read the sentences on page 35. Write T (true), F (false), or ? (not sure). You have four minutes.

My wife and I bought a new house last year. We are happy with the neighborhood. It has good schools and stores nearby, but the house is a little small for our family, so we decided to add to the house–to build an addition.

To change a house in this town, you have to ask permission from a special board, a group of people who control building in the town. We asked for permission from the board and they contacted all the neighbors.

Our neighbors from across the street said no because the placement of the new front door would not be good for Feng Shui. They believe that *chi*, energy, comes in and goes out the front door of a house. The new door on our house would face our neighbors' front door. Our neighbors believe that bad energy would come out our front door and go into their front door across the street.

Well, we went to the board and talked about the problem. The board decided that we couldn't build the addition because it would have a bad effect on the neighborhood. I don't think this is fair. This is my property and I should be able to do what I want with it. I don't believe in Feng Shui. It's an outdated Chinese philosophy from the past. It's not a philosophy for today in my town.

_____ 1. The writer probably has children.

_____ 2. The writer is happy with his house.

_____ 3. The board makes decisions about building.

_____ 4. *Chi* is another word for energy.

_____ 5. According to Feng Shui, bad energy goes out the front door.

_____ 6. The neighbors are Chinese.

_____ 7. The writer is worried about bad energy.

_____ 8. The board believes in Feng Shui.

_____ 9. The writer believes that Feng Shui is important.

_____ 10. The board decided that the writer could build the addition.

C VOCABULARY

Circle the letter of the word or phrase closest in meaning to the boldfaced word(s) in the sentence.

1. The cat **comes in** at night.

   a. steps   **b.** leaves   **c.** enters

2. You need to **ask for** permission from your father to stay out after 10:00 P.M.

   a. tell   **b.** request   **c.** demand

3. You can play outside, but don't **go out of** the yard.

   a. permit   **b.** leave   **c.** stay in

4. I want to build **an addition**.

   a. a better house   **b.** more on to the house   **c.** a higher house

5. This town doesn't have a mayor. It has a **board** that makes decisions.

   a. group   **b.** neighborhood   **c.** control

6. The **placement** of that tree in the yard is not good. It won't get any sun.

   a. location   **b.** height   **c.** outside

7. *Chi* is a kind of **energy**.

   a. music   **b.** power   **c.** noise

8. Building new stores will have a good **effect** on this town.

   a. environment   **b.** result   **c.** experience

9. His clothing is **outdated**.

   a. colorful   **b.** boring   **c.** from the past

10. What is your **philosophy** about life?

    a. belief   **b.** expression   **c.** excitement

What suggestions do you have for the man who wants to build the addition?
Check (✓) the ideas you agree with. Then discuss your ideas with a partner.

_____ He should build the addition anyway.

_____ He should move to a new neighborhood.

_____ He should study more about Feng Shui.

_____ He should contact a lawyer.

_____ He should build his addition on a different side of the house.

_____ He should talk to his neighbors.

_____ He should _____. *(your idea)*

VOCABULARY REVIEW

A Here are words from this chapter that form expressions.

VERBS	OTHER EXPRESSIONS
believe in	across from
come from	all over (the city/country/world)
come/go into (a place)	happy with
come/go out of (a place)	on the (south) side
decide to (do something)	the head of (a family/department/company)
talk about	

Part 1

Complete the sentences with expressions from the box. Part of the expression may already be in the sentence.

1. There are people _____ the country who believe in Feng Shui.

2. When young people get jobs or go to college, they often _____ leave home.

3. Where is the beach? It's _____ the south _____ of the city.

4. She likes to _____ town once a week to shop.

5. What are they going to _____ at the meeting?

6. Her position is very important. She is the _____ of the company.

7. I'm not _____ this new sweater. I'm going to take it back to the store.

8. Do they _____ New York or from someplace else?

9. We're neighbors. His house is _____ mine.

10. I _____ playing hard and working hard. I think that they are both important.

Part 2

The following sentences are not correct. Add the words or phrases from the box to the sentences to make them correct. There may be more than one possible answer.

across	in	out of	with
from	into	to	

1. Marie comes France, doesn't she?

2. Stay nearby. Don't go the yard.

3. The town doesn't believe building big malls.

4. Come the house. It's getting late.

5. I'm happy my new school.

6. We're neighbors. We live from each other.

7. Close the door. The cold air is coming the hallway.

8. We decided buy new property.

Part 3

Use the expressions from the list on page 38 to complete the questions. Then ask a classmate the questions.

1. Who lives _____ you?

2. Are you _____ your work in English? What would you like to improve?

3. What is your philosophy of life? What do you _____?

4. Why did you _____ study English?

B Circle the letter of the word or phrase that best completes each sentence.

1. He's my _____ author. I like his writing style.

   a. natural   **b.** favorite   **c.** safe

2. I can't say that we have a beautiful landscape. We _____ a big building across the street.

   a. face   **b.** control   **c.** find

3. A _____ has many trees.

   a. lawn   **b.** forest   **c.** desert

4. Do you _____ going out to dinner or cooking at home?

   a. find   **b.** prefer   **c.** contact

5. She is only thirty years old, but she is the _____ of a large company.

   a. position   **b.** board   **c.** head

6. When I saw him, he didn't _____ his new job.

   a. mention   **b.** control   **c.** ask for

7. Their house was too small after they had children, so they decided to build a(n) _____ to their house.

   a. landscape   **b.** position   **c.** addition

8. Is the new mall going to have a bad _____ on your neighborhood?

   a. change   **b.** effect   **c.** expression

9. The teacher _____ the students their grades.

   a. contacted   **b.** faced   **c.** showed

10. Feng Shui is the art of the _____ of things.

   a. effect   **b.** changing   **c.** placement

C Match each word to the word or phrase with a similar meaning.

_____	1. favorite	**a.** talk about
_____	2. forest	**b.** top person or front of something
_____	3. property	**c.** lots of trees
_____	4. manager	**d.** landscape
_____	5. head	**e.** within a building
_____	6. face	**f.** preferred
_____	7. mention	**g.** job or place
_____	8. scenery	**h.** building or land
_____	9. position	**i.** person in charge of a group of workers
_____	10. inside	**j.** be in front of

Chapter 3 Working or Overworking?

A FIRST LOOK

A BACKGROUND BUILDING

1. Look at the illustration on page 42. List some differences between this person's real situation and his dream.

In His Real Situation	In His Dream
works in a small cubicle	

2. Work in small groups. Complete these sentences to describe your 'dream jobs'. Your 'dream job' is the perfect job for you.

   a. **Salary:** My salary would be _____.

   b. **Schedule:** I would work from _____ to

   _____.

   c. **Number of vacation days:** I would have _____.

   d. **Benefits** (for example, health insurance, retirement plan, and sick days): I would have _____.

   e. **Perks** (for example, membership in a club, use of a company car): I would have _____.

More Work—True or False?

1   "I work too hard." Does this sound familiar? People in the United States often say this. They complain a lot about overwork, but are they really working too hard?

2   People in the United States do work a few more hours now than they did in 1973. The average workweek went up slightly, 5 from 37.5 hours a week to 39 hours a week. Most people still work from Monday to Friday; they don't have to work on weekends. The workweek is almost the same as it was in 1973.

3   So, why do people think they work more now? Some   10 people do work more. People in their 30s and 40s always work more than when they were younger. People in this age group also worked more hours 30 years ago. People work less only when they are over 50. It's a normal part of work life. The big difference for people is not time at work; it's the time away 15 from work. People spend more time getting to work. The average commute (trip between home and work) has increased by 17.5 percent in the last 20 years. Also, with more women working outside the home, there is more to do at home during non-working hours. "Work" doesn't really end at the office. 20

4   How does this compare to work schedules in other countries? In many countries, people have to work 5.5, 6 or even 7 days a week. In some countries, factories and offices stay open late, but workers have two hours for lunch. In other countries, the regular workday is 8 hours, but workers, 25 especially male workers, don't get home until late at night. They are expected to go out with their co-workers and managers after work.

5   Of course vacations always help! Workers in Spain have the highest average number of paid days off each year (32). Workers in the United States have the fewest (11). However, in some countries, people don't take all their vacation time. In Japan, workers "get" 17.5 days off, but they only take 9. In Great Britain, workers get 28 days off, but only take 20. If workers don't take vacation days off, they are not really vacation days.

30

35

6   Complaining about too much work is probably common all over the world. We all think we have too much to do and, in fact, we probably all do!

C TOPIC

Read the topics below. Match each topic to a paragraph in the reading. Write the number of the paragraph on the line.

_____ vacation time

_____ work schedules in other countries

_____ complaining common everywhere

_____ why people feel overworked

_____ complaints about overwork

_____ the typical work schedule in the United States

SCANNING/VOCABULARY

Part 1

Scan the reading for the word in column A. Write the number of the line where you find the word. Then compare the word in column A to the word(s) in column B. Are the meanings similar or different? Write **S** (similar) or **D** (different) on the line.

A	Line Number	B	S or D?
1. complain		say what's good about something	
2. average		usual	
3. slightly		a lot	
4. normal		usual	
5. commute		trip between work and home	
6. increased		gotten smaller	
7. schedules		times to do things	
8. regular		normal	
9. co-workers		managers	
10. highest		lowest	
11. paid		with money	
12. fewest		most	

Part 2

Complete the sentences with words from the box.

average	complain	got	paid	vacation
compare	expected	normal	took	work

1. The company was celebrating its twenty-fifth anniversary. As a special "thank you" to the employees, everyone _____ the day off.

2. My _____ schedule each day is 8:00 to 5:00.

3. Anna had a bad cold so she _____ the day off.

4. How many days of _____ do you get each year?

5. What time do you go to _____ in the morning?

6. Sometimes I work overtime and sometimes I go home early, but my _____ workday is about eight hours.

7. No one says, "Wear a black suit," but everyone does. We are _____ to wear black suits.

8. I'm not happy about my vacation schedule, but I don't want to _____ because I just started working here a year ago.

9. We can take more days off if we want to, but only ten days are _____ days off.

10. When you _____ our company's benefits with those at other companies, you see that they are about the same.

Circle the letter of the answer that best completes each sentence.

1. In 1973, people in the U.S. worked an average of _____ hours.

   a. 37   **b.** 37.5   **c.** 39

2. Most people in the U.S. _____ on weekends.

   a. have to work   **b.** like to work   **c.** don't work

3. On average, people in the U.S. spend _____ time at work now than they used to.

   a. less   **b.** a little more   **c.** the same amount of

4. People in the U.S. now spend _____ time getting to work.

   a. less   **b.** more   **c.** the same amount of

5. A two-hour lunch break is _____ in the U.S.

   a. typical   **b.** uncommon   **c.** average

6. According to the reading, someone who is 35 probably works _____ someone who is 55.

   a. less than   **b.** more than   **c.** the same amount as

7. People in the U.S. feel that they work more because of the way they spend their time _____.

   a. outside of work   **b.** on vacation   **c.** at work

8. People between 30 and 50 work more than older people. This is _____ it used to be.

    a. the same as   **b.** more than   **c.** different from the way

9. The main difference in work schedules around the world is _____.

    a. the number of days worked   **b.** the time that work ends   **c.** both a and b

10. According to the reading, people in the U.S. _____ vacation days than people in Japan.

    a. take fewer   **b.** take more   **c.** get more

LOOK AGAIN

A VOCABULARY

Circle the letter of the word or phrase that best completes each sentence.

1. Her face is _____ to me, but I can't remember how I know her.

    a. familiar   **b.** regular   **c.** normal

2. They changed our pay _____. It went from $5.15 an hour to $5.25 an hour.

    a. slightly   **b.** normally   **c.** especially

3. The _____ decides on our schedules for the month.

    a. researcher   **b.** manager   **c.** worker

4. The company is doing well. Sales _____ last year.

    a. averaged   **b.** expected   **c.** increased

5. I have a short _____. It only takes me fifteen minutes to get there.

    a. commute   **b.** office   **c.** schedule

6. Activities _____ gardening and cooking are relaxing.

    a. about   **b.** especially   **c.** such as

7. Taking a vacation in the summer is _____ in many countries.

    a. not allowed   **b.** common   **c.** average

8. _____ workers are paid more than women workers.

    a. Factory   **b.** Male   **c.** Office

9. One bad thing about my new job is that I have _____ vacation days than I did at my old job.

    a. fewer   **b.** more   **c.** five more

10. I can't remember exactly how much dinner was, but it was _____ fifty dollars.

    a. about   **b.** like   **c.** regular

B READING COMPREHENSION

Find the answers to the following questions in the reading. Underline them in the reading and write the number of the question next to them.

1. About how many hours a week do people in the United States work on average?

2. Do most people work on weekends in the United States?

3. What are two reasons why people feel they work more?

4. How many paid vacation days do people in Spain have on average?

5. In Japan, how many days of vacation do people take?

6. How many days of vacation do people get in Japan?

Read the chart and answer the questions that follow.

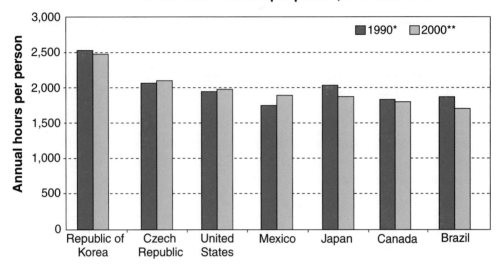

Annual hours worked per person, 1990 and 2000

*1991: Germany; 1993: Czech Republic.
**1998: Canada; 1999: Japan, United Kingdom and Brazil.

1. In which two countries did people work the most hours in 2000?

2. Which country had the lowest average work hours?

3. In which countries did the number of hours worked increase in the ten-year period?

4. Which two countries had the biggest decrease in hours worked?

5. Were you surprised by any of the information in this chart?

◆D◆ THINK ABOUT IT

Discuss the questions in a small group.

1. The chart on page 51 shows the average number of hours people in some countries work per year. How many hours do people you know work each week? Do they have more work to do at home than people had in the past? Have their commutes increased?

2. How many days of vacation do people usually get in your country? How many days of vacation do you think a company should give its employees?

3. There are 120 hours during the workweek, from Monday until Friday. How do you spend your time? Complete the chart and compare your schedule with a friend's or a classmate's.

Time Spent	M	T	W	TH	F	Total Hours
Sleeping						
Working						
Studying						
Cooking/Eating						
Commuting						
Work at home						
Free time						
Total						120

A BACKGROUND BUILDING

Discuss these questions about the picture.

1. Where is the man in the picture?

2. What is he thinking about?

Read the passage. Then read the sentences on page 55. Write T (true), F (false), or ? (not sure). You have four minutes.

I used to complain about working too much. I almost never took vacations. I worked about sixty hours a week and often had to travel out of town. I got very tired of sleeping in hotels and waiting in airports. I saw so little of my children that they didn't even know when I was out of town.

Now, however, I'd be happy to be overworked. I'd be happy to have *any* work. After twenty-four years, my company laid me off. It wasn't because I didn't do a good job; I was one of their best workers. They just had too many workers and business was bad, so they laid off thirty people. They call it *downsizing*.

I can't explain how bad I feel. I'm terribly embarrassed because I don't have a job. I don't want my neighbors to see me at home during the day. I'm worried because I'm not making any money to support my family. I'm also lonely because I don't see my co-workers anymore. I used to look forward to retirement, but now that I have free time, I don't know what to do with myself.

I'm looking for another job, but it's hard. I didn't need to use a computer in my old job and I never learned any other skills. I only speak one language. I think companies want to hire younger workers. I don't want to get another job. I want my old job back.

_____ 1. The writer is probably young.

_____ 2. *Downsizing* means "make smaller."

_____ 3. The writer didn't do a good job when he was working.

_____ 4. The writer worked for his company for a long time.

_____ 5. The writer used to spend a lot of time with his children.

_____ 6. He has a lot of job skills.

_____ 7. He doesn't want his neighbors to know that he was laid off.

_____ 8. He still spends time with his co-workers.

_____ 9. He is the only one who lost his job at his company.

_____ 10. He knows a second language.

C VOCABULARY

Circle the letter of the word or phrase closest in meaning to the boldfaced word(s).

1. The company **laid off** a lot of people.
   a. no longer had work for
   b. gave time off to
   c. gave jobs to

2. I'm **tired of** this weather.
   a. excited about
   b. happy with
   c. unhappy with

3. We work six days **a week**.
   a. every week
   b. this week
   c. all week

4. I didn't go **out of town** on my vacation.
   a. nearby
   b. downtown
   c. to another city

5. I know all my **neighbors**.
   a. co-workers
   b. friends
   c. people who live nearby

6. It's hard to **support** a family of four on my salary.

    a. hold up   **b.** take out   **c.** pay living costs for

7. I want to **look for** a new job.

    a. try   **b.** try to find   **c.** get

8. It's very **hard** to work at two jobs.

    a. difficult   **b.** strong   **c.** soft

9. My company **hires** more people in the summer.

    a. gives jobs to   **b.** uses   **c.** lays off

10. What do you plan to do in your **retirement**?

    a. time after you stop working   **b.** vacation   **c.** time off

D REACT

Answer the questions. Then discuss your answers with your classmates.

1. In the timed reading, the man is very unhappy. What suggestions do you have for him? Check (✓) the ideas you agree with. Then discuss your ideas with a partner.

_____ He should spend time with his old co-workers.

_____ He should spend time with other people who were laid off.

_____ He should go to see a doctor about his unhappiness.

_____ He should continue to stay at home.

_____ He should leave the house every day as if he still had a job.

_____ He should tell his neighbors he is looking for a new job.

_____ He should _____. *(your idea)*

2. Do you think this man can develop new skills? Is it a good idea for him to try? If so, what skills would help him? Make a list on a separate piece of paper. Then compare your list with a classmate's.

VOCABULARY REVIEW

A Here are words from this chapter that form expressions.

VERBS		OTHER EXPRESSIONS
complain about	look for	an average of*
go out with	look forward to	compared to
have a/the day off	take/have a vacation	on average*
lay off (workers)	worry about	sure about
		tired of

*NOTE: Here are some examples of how to use *on average* and *an average of*.

I study *an average of* four hours a day.

On average, I study four hours a day.

Part 1

Complete the sentences with expressions from the box. Part of the expression may already be in the sentence.

1. Sam is starting to _____ his job. He is afraid he might lose it.

2. We sometimes work long days, but _____ we only work 7.5 hours a day.

3. I'm _____ working so hard. I need to _____ a vacation!

4. I work six days a week. I _____ on Sunday, so I _____ it all week long.

5. My company is going to _____ 200 people next month. I think I will _____ a new job just in case I'm one of those 200 people.

6. I don't like to go out with my co-workers because they just _____ our jobs all the time. It's boring to listen to them.

7. On Friday nights I often _____ my friends.

8. I work _____ thirty-seven hours a week. This is not too much _____ work hours in some companies.

9. Are you _____ the time? I thought the meeting started at 7:30, not 8:00.

Part 2

The following sentences are not correct. Add a word from the box to each sentence to make it correct. There may be more than one possible answer.

about	of	off	on	to	with

1. I'm looking forward vacation.

2. I complain the problem, but nothing happens.

3. The company laid thirty people last month.

4. Are you going out your friends tonight?

5. They work an average eight hours a day.

6. We don't have a regular schedule, but people work thirty-five hours a week average.

7. He's worried his job.

8. I'm not sure his age. I think he's about 40.

9. Ten hours of work is a long day compared the hours people work in some countries.

10. I'm tired working so hard.

Part 3

Ask a classmate the questions below.

1. What do you sometimes complain about?

2. Do you ever worry about anything? If so, what?

3. On average, how much time do you spend doing homework?

4. Do you work? If so, when do you work?

5. Do you ever feel lucky compared to other people? If so, when?

6. What is something you are looking forward to?

7. Do you know anyone who lost a job because the company laid off people?

8. What day of the week is the best to have off from work? Why?

Circle the letter of the word or phrase that best completes the sentence.

1. Last year I _____ a two-week vacation.
   a. took   **b.** worked   **c.** made

2. My company _____ a lot of people from that university.
   a. does   **b.** lays off   **c.** hires

3. My salary is very low. I don't make enough money to _____ myself very well.
   a. take   **b.** have   **c.** support

4. I plan to _____ when I'm 55.
   a. be laid off   **b.** retire   **c.** tire

5. I can't _____ a job until I finish my exams.
   a. compare   **b.** look for   **c.** hire

6. When the company lost money, they _____ thirty people.
   a. hired   **b.** took   **c.** laid off

7. The people who live near me are my _____.
   a. neighbors   **b.** co-workers   **c.** workers

8. My manager _____ me to do a good job.
   a. takes   **b.** tries   **c.** expects

9. I worked ten hours one day, but only six the next. I worked an _____ of eight hours.
   a. average   **b.** workload   **c.** schedule

10. It took an hour to get our food at the restaurant, so I _____ to the manager.
    a. retired   **b.** complained   **c.** expected

C **Match each word to the word or phrase with a similar meaning.**

_____ 1. regular

_____ 2. average

_____ 3. free time

_____ 4. hard

_____ 5. try to find

_____ 6. vacation

_____ 7. workers

_____ 8. hire

_____ 9. co-workers

_____ 10. support

a. paid time off work

b. give a job to

c. people you work with

d. normal

e. look for

f. time when you are not working or studying

g. usual

h. take care of

i. difficult

j. employees

Chapter 4
What's a Family?

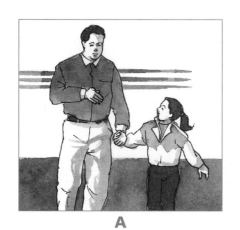

A

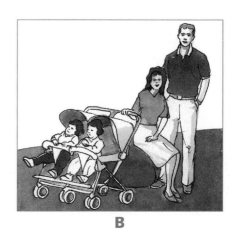

B

C

D

A FIRST LOOK

A BACKGROUND BUILDING

Answer the questions below. Then compare your answers with a classmate's.

1. Look at the pictures on page 62. Describe the people that you see.

   _____

   _____

   _____

   _____

2. Which pictures show families? Why do you think so?

   _____

   _____

   _____

   _____

3. What is a family? Write your definition below.

   _____

   _____

   _____

   _____

What Is a Family?

1   Every ten years, the government of the United States counts its population. This is called a census. The government wants to know about Americans. It wants to know where people live, what kind of work they do, and what they do in their free time. It also wants to know if they are married, single, 5 or divorced, and if they have children.

2   The government uses the word *household* to describe a group of people living together. Some people live with their families. Some live alone. Others live with friends or partners. All of these are households. 10

3   In the 2000 census, there were almost 105 million households. Only 25 percent of these households had families with a married husband and wife with their own children. What does this number show?

4   First, not as many people are married. Some people today 15 don't feel they have to get married. Some are waiting until they are older to get married. Others haven't found the right person to marry. Some people prefer to live alone. Single mothers are more common now. There are more single fathers today as well. Some of these parents never married. Others married 20 and then divorced.

5   There are also a number of households with husbands and wives but no children. Some married people may choose not to have children. Others may have some difficulty having children. Many have adult children who live on their own. 25

6   The census shows many types of households in the United States. This brings up a question: Are the new households changing the definition of *family*?

◆ C ▸ TOPIC

Read the topics below. Match each topic to a paragraph in the reading. Write the number of the paragraph on the line.

_____ why fewer people are married

_____ a change in the definition of *family*

_____ an explanation of the U.S. census

_____ reasons people don't have children in the household

_____ information about households

_____ a definition of *household*

D SCANNING/VOCABULARY

Part 1

Scan the reading for the word in column A. Write the number of the line where you find the word. Then compare the word in column A to the word in column B. Are the meanings similar or different? Write **S** (similar) or **D** (different) on the line.

A	Line Number	B	S or D?
1. counts		connects	
2. population		number of people in a place	
3. census		count of the population	
4. married		single	
5. divorced		married	
6. alone		with friends	
7. own		another person's	
8. common		unusual	
9. choose		decide	
10. adult		young	
11. types		kinds	
12. definition		meaning	

Part 2

Complete the sentences with words from the box.

adults	count	difficulty	household	own
census	definition	divorced	married	type

1. Little children usually learn to _____ using their fingers.

2. You don't need to drive me. I have my _____ car.

3. A man who has a wife is _____ .

4. The average _____ in the United States has 2.6 people.

5. They're not children anymore. All three of them are _____.

6. They are no longer married. They are _____.

7. I'm having some _____ with this key. Can you try to unlock the door?

8. The _____ shows the population in each part of the country.

9. I don't know the _____ of this word. Could I use your dictionary?

10. What _____ of restaurant would you like to go to?

E ▸ READING COMPREHENSION

Circle the letter of the word or phrase that best completes each sentence.

1. The U.S. government will take the next census _____.

   a. in ten years **b.** next year **c.** in 2010

2. In the census, the government wants to _____ its people.

   a. go to **b.** learn about **c.** decide for

3. A household has many different forms. People can live in households with their families, alone, or with a _____.

   a. friend **b.** husband **c.** child

4. Of the 105 million households that were in the United States in 2000, _____ 25 percent had husbands and wives.

   a. only **b.** more than **c.** less than

5. In the 2000 census, about _____ households did not have a husband, a wife, and their own children.

   a. 26 million **b.** 79 million **c.** 105 million

6. Today there are many reasons why not as many people are married: They haven't found the right partner; they don't feel that they have to get married; or they like being _____.

   a. married **b.** divorced **c.** alone

7. Some single parents married and then divorced. Others _____.

   a. are alone **b.** never married **c.** are divorced

8. In paragraph 5, there are _____ reasons why husbands and wives don't have children in their households.

   a. two **b.** three **c.** four

9. Some husbands and wives no longer have children at home because their own children are _____.

   a. young **b.** adults **c.** single

10. Because there are so many different kinds of households, we may ask a question about _____ *family*.

    a. the meaning of **b.** the number of people in a **c.** the household of a

LOOK AGAIN

A VOCABULARY

Circle the letter of the word that best completes each sentence.

1. Single parents are more _____ than they used to be.
   a. familiar   b. common   c. right

2. What is the _____ of Los Angeles?
   a. count   b. census   c. population

3. Can you give me a _____ for the word *government*?
   a. census   b. count   c. definition

4. A _____ means a group of people who live together.
   a. apartment   b. house   c. household

5. I'm single. I've never been _____.
   a. divorced   b. married   c. changed

6. I don't rent an apartment. I have my _____ home.
   a. only   b. right   c. own

7. That's my _____ over there, the one in the red dress.
   a. husband   b. wife   c. son

8. She's 45. She is not a(n) _____.
   a. adult   b. child   c. woman

9. Through the census, the U.S. government _____ and describes the population.
   a. chooses   b. decides   c. counts

10. What _____ of man do you want to marry?
    a. husband   b. type   c. definition

B ▶ READING COMPREHENSION

Find the answers to the questions in the reading. Underline the answers and write the number of the question next to them.

1. What is the counting of the population called?

2. How often does the U.S. government take the census?

3. In the 2000 census, what were 25 percent of the households?

4. What is one reason why not as many people are married now as in the past?

5. What is one reason why husbands and wives don't have children in their households?

6. What might be changing because of the many types of households in the United States?

C ▶ READING FOR SPECIFIC INFORMATION

Read the paragraph and then complete the chart that follows.

The census shows the change in the population. It is interesting to compare one census to the next because the census happens every ten years. For example, in the 1980 census, 66 percent of the adults (18 and older) in the U.S. were married. In 1990, 62 percent were married, and in 2000, 60 percent. The census also shows the percentage of those who were never married. In 2000, it was 23 percent; in 1990, 22 percent; and in 1980, 20 percent. In 1980, 6 percent of adults were divorced; in 1990 it was 8 percent; and in 2000, it increased to 10 percent.

Finally, there are widowed people, those whose husbands or wives died. They were 8 percent of the population in 1980, the same in 1990, and 7 percent in 2000.

There is a story in these census numbers. They show us changes in our population and in society.

Marital Status of Population 18 and Older			
	1980	1990	2000
Never Married		22%	23%
Married	66%		60%
Widowed	8%		7%
Divorced		8%	
	100%	100%	100%

SOURCE: U.S. Census Bureau, Statistical Abstracts of the United States, 2001.

D THINK ABOUT IT

Answer the questions. Then compare your answers with a classmate's.

1. How many different censuses are there on the chart in Part C?

2. How much time is covered by this chart?

3. Did the percentage of people who have never been married go up or go down between 1980 and 2000?

4. In terms of the census, are widowed people married?

5. Did the number of widowed people go up or go down between 1980 and 2000?

6. Why do you think the percentage of married people went down between 1980 and 2000?

A POINT OF VIEW

A ▶ BACKGROUND BUILDING

Work in a small group. Look at the picture and discuss the questions.

1. How do you think the people in the picture are related?

2. What does the older couple hope for?

Read the passage. Then read the sentences on page 74. Write T (true), F (false), or ? (not sure). You have four minutes.

My daughter came to my wife and me the other day to say that she wants to live with her boyfriend. I said that would be fine as soon as they get married. She said that they don't want to get married. They want to live together without getting married. I said, "No way!"

Linda, my daughter, is intelligent and has a lot of common sense. She is 28 and she has a good job in a computer company. Her boyfriend, Frank, is a nice guy. He works for the government. He has a good job, too. They make a nice couple. But I think that it is a mistake for young people to set up a household without getting married. They need to be husband and wife before they live together.

My wife and I will pay for the wedding. We'll have a nice party and we'll even send them on a honeymoon to Hawaii.

Linda says that too many people are getting married and then divorced. She and Frank want to be sure that they are right for each other. I don't think it's right. I don't understand why they don't want to get married. They are both single and the right age to get married. I'd really like to have some grandchildren.

I won't change my mind about this. Living together without getting married is just wrong, and no daughter of mine is going to live with a man without tying the knot.

_____ 1. Linda is the writer's daughter.

_____ 2. Linda is Frank's girlfriend.

_____ 3. Linda is 21.

_____ 4. Frank is older than Linda.

_____ 5. Linda works for the government.

_____ 6. Linda and Frank want to get married.

_____ 7. Linda and Frank want to live together.

_____ 8. The writer will not pay for the wedding or the honeymoon.

_____ 9. The writer will change his mind.

_____ 10. The writer doesn't want his daughter to become a wife.

C VOCABULARY

Circle the letter of the word or phrase closest in meaning to the boldfaced word(s) in the sentence.

1. He has a **daughter** and two sons.
   - **a.** young child
   - **b.** male child
   - **c.** female child

2. They want to have a party **without** spending a lot of money.
   - **a.** and not be
   - **b.** and also be
   - **c.** and enjoy

3. **That couple** is really happy together. They should get married.
   - **a.** That husband and wife
   - **b.** That partnership
   - **c.** Those two people

4. It's a **mistake** to get married very young.
   - **a.** right idea
   - **b.** bad idea
   - **c.** good idea

5. They are planning to **set up** their household in the town where they grew up.
   - **a.** put
   - **b.** start
   - **c.** show up

6. They had a long **honeymoon**.

   a. wedding trip   **b.** wedding   **c.** wedding party

7. That husband and wife are **right for each other**.

   a. kind   **b.** correct   **c.** good partners

8. Your answers on this test are all **wrong**.

   a. confusing   **b.** right   **c.** incorrect

9. He's always **changing his mind**.

   a. having a different idea   **b.** shaking his head   **c.** sharing his ideas

10. They are going to **tie the knot**.

   a. go on a honeymoon   **b.** have a big wedding   **c.** get married

D REACT

Answer the questions. Then discuss your answers with a classmate.

1. Do you know any people who live together and are not married? If so, why did the couple choose not to get married?

2. You know how Linda's father feels about Linda and Frank living together. How do you think Linda's other family members feel about it? How do you think Frank's family feels about it?

3. What would you say to the father in the reading? Put a check (✓) next to your answer(s).

_____ Don't worry. They will get married later.

_____ Many couples don't get married today.

_____ Your daughter is an adult. She can do what she wants.

_____ Don't give them any money until they get married.

_____ Don't talk to your daughter until she and her boyfriend get married.

_____ _____. *(your idea)*

VOCABULARY REVIEW

 A Here are words from this chapter that form expressions.

VERBS		OTHER EXPRESSIONS
change (one's) mind	live on (one's) own	every day/week/month/year
get a job	live with (someone)	kind/type of
get married/divorced	pay for (something)	married/divorced
live in (a place)	work for (a company)	percent of (something)

Part 1

Complete the sentences with expressions from the box. Part of the expression may already be in the sentence.

1. They _____ Japan now. They moved there last year.

2. Let's go out for lunch. I'll _____ it.

3. I didn't have a day off last week. I worked _____.

4. Do you think she will feel lonely if she lives _____?

5. When do they plan to _____? They have been together for many years.

6. I used to _____ a large company, but I didn't like it so I quit. Now I'm trying to _____ at a small company.

7. You can never be sure with her parents. They often _____ about things.

8. What _____ U.S. households have children?

9. I know they were not happy together. Are they _____ now?

10. What _____ car do you drive?

Part 2

The following sentences are not correct. Add the words from the box to the sentences to make them correct. There may be more than one possible answer.

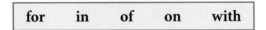

| for | in | of | on | with |

1. He's not living his wife now. They're probably going to get divorced.

2. In 2000, 48 percent all households were unmarried people.

3. What kind dog do you have?

4. They don't live their own house. They rent an apartment.

5. He doesn't live with anyone. He lives his own.

6. I forgot to bring money to pay lunch.

7. What is the definition the word *widowed*?

8. Are there a lot of students living this neighborhood?

9. He worked that company for twenty years.

10. A honeymoon is a special type trip.

Part 3

Use the expressions from the list on page 76 to complete the questions. Then ask a classmate the questions.

1. Do you live _____ or with someone else?

2. If you are not _____ already, do you want to _____ someday, or do you want to stay single?

3. Do you _____, or do you have a business of your own?

4. When a man and a woman go out to eat, who do you think should _____ the meal?

5. How often do you see your family? _____

B Circle the letter of the word or phrase that best completes each sentence.

1. He never married. He's _____.
   a. divorced   **b.** single   **c.** alone

2. She's having a lot of _____ with her job. It's not easy.
   a. difficulty   **b.** meaning   **c.** schedules

3. They each have their _____ cars because the husband works on the north side of the city and the wife works on the south side.
   a. own   **b.** connection to   **c.** shared

4. Divorce is more _____ now than it was during the last census.
   a. average   **b.** common   **c.** voluntary

5. Once a week I go to church. I go _____ Sunday.
   a. all   **b.** every   **c.** for

6. When a person's husband or wife dies, they are _____.
   a. divorced   **b.** single   **c.** widowed

7. She's not your type. Are you sure that she will be the right _____ for you?

    a. husband   **b.** wife   **c.** wedding

8. It's your decision. Which do you _____?

    a. choose   **b.** define   **c.** fail

9. The government _____ the population with the census.

    a. counts   **b.** knows   **c.** prefers

10. No, they're not married. They are living _____.

    a. in a household   **b.** together   **c.** without

C   **Match each word to the word or phrase with a similar meaning.**

_____	1. own	**a.** correct
_____	2. wife	**b.** kinds
_____	3. common	**c.** count of people
_____	4. population	**d.** usual
_____	5. definition	**e.** female marriage partner
_____	6. types	**f.** not a child
_____	7. right	**g.** number of people in a place
_____	8. census	**h.** not another's
_____	9. couple	**i.** meaning
_____	10. adult	**j.** two people

Chapter 5
Technology: Changing Our Lives

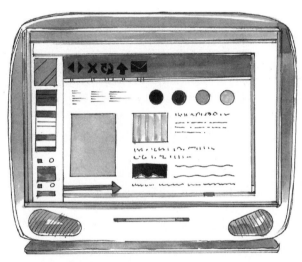

A FIRST LOOK

A BACKGROUND BUILDING

1. Look at the pictures on page 80. How is the World Wide Web like a spider's web?
2. Answer the questions in the survey. Then compare your answers with a classmate's.

Internet Survey

1. Do you use the internet?

   _____ Yes   _____ No

2. Where do you use the Internet? Check (✓) your answers.

   _____ at school   _____ at a friend's house

   _____ at home   _____ at a cyber cafe

   _____ at the office   _____ on a hand-held device

   _____ at the library

3. How many times a week do you go online?

   _____ once   _____ three times

   _____ twice   _____ every day

4. What do you do online?

   _____ check e-mail   _____ visit chat rooms

   _____ do instant messaging _____ search for information

   _____ play games   _____ surf the Web*

*visit many different Web sites

Online

1   "Go online." "Surf the net." "Do a Web search." These expressions didn't exist just a few years ago. But the Internet has changed our way of communicating and getting information. We log on. We go online. We e-mail each other. Then we search for information as we surf the World Wide   5
Web.

2   How did the Internet start? It was developed in the late 1960s with support from the Defense Department of the United States. Researchers needed a way to communicate with each other. A computer network was the solution for them. From   10
this early work came the Internet, connections between computers. The World Wide Web came in the 1980s. The "Web" is a system that makes it easy to see and use information on the Internet. Most of the time, Web sites are on the Internet, but there are also local sites, for example,   15
within a business. This is called an intranet.

3   At one time, people had to find information in books, journals, and newspapers. They had to visit libraries. With an Internet connection, people no longer need to go to libraries for information. They can access the Internet on their cell   20
phones or laptops. They can sit in their own homes and have the world come to them.

4   Of course, the Internet has its problems as well. First, some people are not able to use the Internet because they don't

have access to it. For many, it is too expensive. For others, the 25
technology is not available where they live. Also, the Internet
system sometimes doesn't work because too many people are
using it at once or because of technical problems.

5   On the other hand, access to the Internet is improving.
Many libraries, even in small towns, now have Internet access 30
for the public. New technology has also reduced many
problems with the Internet.

6   Internet use is very popular among young people. They
realize how easy it is to find the information they need quickly
on the Web. Most young people are comfortable with the 35
Internet and use it often. They no longer spend hours
researching in libraries. They can log on anywhere.

C TOPIC

**Read the topics below. Match each topic to a paragraph in the reading.
Write the number of the paragraph on the line.**

_____ the Internet is a place to find information

_____ young people and the Internet

_____ more people have access and fewer problems online

_____ new vocabulary related to the Internet

_____ the Internet is not perfect

_____ the history of the Internet

Part 1

Scan the reading for the word in column A. Write the number of the line where you find the word. Then compare the word in column A to the word(s) in column B. Are the meanings similar or different? Write **S** (similar) or **D** (different) on the line.

A	Line Number	B	S or D?
1. log on		stop working on a computer	
2. search		try to find	
3. developed		ended	
4. support		help	
5. communicate		talk	
6. network		group of connections	
7. solution		problem	
8. access		get to; the ability to get to	
9. laptop		small phone	
10. (the) public		people	
11. reduced		made bigger	
12. realize		understand	

Part 2

Complete the sentences with words from the box.

access	exist	reduce	solution	system
develop	information	search	support	work

1. That computer company offers technical _____ for its customers by telephone.

2. What's the _____ to this problem?

3. It is easy to find _____ on the Internet.

4. A family has to _____ spending in order to save money.

5. Libraries give the public _____ to books, newspapers, computers, and often the Internet.

6. When the company's network doesn't _____ well, using the Internet is very difficult.

7. The company spent a lot of money on a new computer _____, but it is very slow.

8. It's strange to think that the World Wide Web did not _____ a short time ago.

9. I'm not going to rent just any apartment. I'm going to _____ until I find the right place to live.

10. There are plans to _____ the old part of town. There will be new stores and restaurants on Main Street.

E ► READING COMPREHENSION

Circle the letter of the word or phrase that best completes each sentence.

1. "Go online" and "surf the net" are examples of _____ used to talk about the Internet.

   a. getting
   information
   b. new language
   c. Web mail

2. The Internet was developed _____ the Web.

   a. when
   b. before
   c. after

3. The Internet was developed because researchers wanted _____.

   a. better
   communication
   b. government
   support
   c. local sites

4. Before the Internet, it was _____ to get information.

   a. easier
   b. more difficult
   c. impossible

5. *They can have the world come to them* (paragraph 3) means that they can get information wherever they _____.

   a. research
   b. communicate
   c. are

6. _____ is an Internet problem *not* mentioned by the author.

   a. Access
   b. Support
   c. Expense

7. New technology has _____ access to the Internet.

   a. increased
   b. decreased
   c. shared

8. Internet access in libraries is an example of _____ use.

   a. popular
   b. private
   c. public

9. Young people like the Internet because it is easy and _____

   a. comfortable
   b. quick
   c. popular

10. The Internet is a _____ system, and the Web is an information system.

    a. knowledge
    b. technology
    c. communication

A ▸ VOCABULARY

Circle the letter of the word or phrase that best completes each sentence.

1. I'm flying from New York to Saudi Arabia with a _____ in London.
   a. network   **b.** communication   **c.** connection

2. His family is important in his life. They give him a lot of _____.
   a. solutions   **b.** support   **c.** expressions

3. The Wright Brothers were the first to _____ a flying machine.
   a. realize   **b.** develop   **c.** believe in

4. The telephone system is a _____ for communication.
   a. network   **b.** sales   **c.** technology

5. I'm studying computer _____. I want to get a job working on computer systems.
   a. information   **b.** sales   **c.** technology

6. I brought my _____ with me so that I could do some work on the plane.
   a. Internet   **b.** laptop   **c.** network

7. He's on a diet. He needs to _____ the amount of food he eats.
   a. realize   **b.** reduce   **c.** access

8. I can't find a good Vietnamese restaurant in this city. One doesn't _____.
   a. reduce   **b.** exist   **c.** create

9. If you don't know his address, you can _____ for it on the Web.
   a. communicate   **b.** share   **c.** search

10. Every morning I _____ and check my e-mail before I do anything else.
    a. log on   **b.** develop   **c.** reduce

B ▶ READING COMPREHENSION

Read the passage on pages 82–83 again. Complete the summary of the reading with words or phrases from the box.

access	computers	information	public	search for
communicate	developed	phone	researchers	system

In the 1960s _____ wanted a better way to
(1)

_____. Therefore, they _____ a computer
(2)   (3)

network that later became the Internet. The Internet is a

_____ of communication between _____.
(4)   (5)

The World Wide Web came in the 1980s. The Web is a system that

helps us see and use _____ on the Internet. The Web has
(6)

grown, and many people use the Internet at home or in

_____ places like libraries.
(7)

In the past, people had to go to libraries to _____
(8)

information, but now they can _____ the Web from a
(9)

home computer, a laptop, or a cell _____.
(10)

READING FOR SPECIFIC INFORMATION

Look at the following information about the use of the Internet. Then answer the questions that follow the chart.

Adults in the U.S. Who Went Online in the Last 30 Days		
Age Group	**Number of People**	**Percentage of Age Group**
18–24	25,691,000	58.7
25–34	39,066,000	53.3
35–44	44,791,000	54.8
45–54	34,744,000	40.0
55–64	22,711,000	35.1
65+	32,404,000	10.7
Total (18 and older)	**199,438,000**	**45.4**
SOURCE: U.S. Statistical Abstracts, 2000		

1. What age group has the largest number of Internet users?

   _____

2. Which group had the highest percentage of Internet users?

   _____

3. Why are the answers to numbers 1 and 2 different?

   _____

4. Which group has the smallest number of Internet users?

   _____

5. Write two statements about the information on the graph.

   EXAMPLE: Less than half of the total population went online in the last thirty days.

   1. _____

   2. _____

Read the story and answer the questions that follow.

As you know, cell phones are getting smaller and smaller. I heard a story the other day about a businessman and his cell phone. It seems that he woke up early one morning to the sound of his cell phone ringing. He reached to the table next to his bed, but the phone wasn't there. He kept hearing the ringing, but it sounded far away. Suddenly he realized that the sound was coming from his dog, a Saint Bernard. He then realized that the dog had eaten his phone.

He rushed the dog to the veterinarian and the dog had surgery to remove the phone. Even when the phone was removed from the dog's stomach, it continued ringing. When the doctor finally answered the phone, it was the wrong number.

1. Why did the man wake up?

2. Where was the man's cell phone?

3. What did the man do next?

4. What happened when the doctor answered the call?

5. Do you think that this is a true story? Why or why not?

A BACKGROUND BUILDING

Look at the picture and discuss the questions with a partner.

1. Where are these people?

2. Read the words in the speech balloon. Do you think that this conversation is important? Why or why not?

3. Do you think this woman is doing something wrong?

B TIMED READING

Read the passage. Then read the sentences. Write T (true), F (false), or ? (not sure). You have four minutes.

Cell phones are everywhere: in cars, in restaurants, at concerts, and even on the subway. I worry a lot about drivers who use cell phones. They pay more attention to the telephone conversations that they are having than to the drivers around them. When they are on the phone, they are not concentrating on other cars, making turns, or stopping at red lights. They are really dangerous.

Talking on a cell phone in a public place may not be as dangerous, but it is annoying. I don't understand why, but when people are on the phone, they are loud, much louder than they are in face-to-face conversations. Even worse, people discuss very personal subjects that I don't want to know about. For example, the other day, I was going home on the bus and I heard a phone ringing. The passenger in the seat behind me took out her cell phone and answered. "Yes, they had a good time at the party last night." "Of course, Ricky was there." "Oh, no, he was with Susan." "Oh, didn't you hear? He broke up with Marlene."

I had to listen to these personal details about people that I don't know and don't care about. I finally got so tired of this conversation that I got up, got off the bus, and walked the rest of the way home. I wanted to have a little peace and quiet.

_____ 1. The writer is young.

_____ 2. The writer has a cell phone.

_____ 3. The writer is a good driver.

_____ 4. The writer was on a bus.

_____ 5. The writer was talking on the phone.

_____ 6. A young man answered the cell phone.

_____ 7. The writer enjoyed the conversation.

_____ 8. The conversation was about a party.

_____ 9. The writer thinks that cell-phone use in public places is dangerous.

_____ 10. The writer decided to walk home.

◆ C VOCABULARY

Circle the letter of the word or phrase closest in meaning to the boldfaced word(s).

1. I need a quiet place where I can **concentrate on** my work.
   a. feel upset about
   b. think carefully about
   c. forget about

2. Please **pay attention** when you are in class; don't talk to the person next to you.
   a. say what you think
   b. care a lot about
   c. listen carefully

3. The music was so **loud** that I had to leave.
   a. relaxing
   b. noisy
   c. calm

4. She was a **passenger** in the car at the time of the accident.
   a. driver
   b. rider
   c. helper

5. Cell phones are **everywhere**, so it is hard to avoid them.
   a. in all places
   b. dangerous
   c. annoying

6. We had a long **conversation** on the telephone.

   a. network   **b.** talk   **c.** service

7. Her description of the beach has a lot of **details**. You can picture it easily.

   a. knowledge   **b.** vocabulary   **c.** information

8. Watch out. That dog **is dangerous**.

   a. may hurt you   **b.** is annoying   **c.** is crazy

9. That's a **personal** problem. I don't want a lot of people to know about it.

   a. public   **b.** special   **c.** private

10. He **got off** the plane before they closed the door.

   a. entered   **b.** left   **c.** walked to

D ▶ REACT

Some cities in the United States do not allow drivers to use "hand-held" cell phones when they are driving. What do you think about this? Write two reasons why using a cell phone when driving is *not* a good idea.

1. _____

2. _____

Write two reasons why using a cell phone when driving is a good idea.

1. _____

2. _____

Discuss your ideas with a classmate.

VOCABULARY REVIEW

A Here are words from this chapter that form expressions.

VERBS			
concentrate on	listen to	pay attention to	talk on the phone
get tired of	log on	search for	wake up
go online		spend time	

Part 1

Complete the sentences with expressions from the box.

1. I don't have time to do research in the library, so I'm going to
_____ the information on the Internet.

2. There's a computer over there. You can use my name and password
to _____.

3. There was some problem with our computer network yesterday, so I
couldn't _____ to look for that information.

4. When the computer is slow, I _____ just wasting time,
so I go and do something else.

5. I _____ music on radio stations that I find on the
Internet.

6. There was too much noise at home last night. I couldn't
_____ my homework.

7. There's a great show on TV tonight, so I hope I don't have to
_____ a lot of _____ on homework.

8. Can drivers _____ while they're driving
in your country, or is it against the law?

9. I didn't hear the alarm clock this morning, so I didn't
_____ on time.

10. Please be quiet. It's hard to _____ the teacher
when you're talking to me.

Part 2

The following sentences are not correct. Add the words from the box to the sentences to make them correct. There may be more than one possible answer.

for	of	on	to	up

1. Once you log, the world comes to you.

2. I woke at 6:00 this morning.

3. You should concentrate studying for your test.

4. I searched his address on the Internet, but I couldn't

find it.

5. I wasn't paying attention my friend and I didn't hear what

   she said.

6. They were talking the phone.

7. Do you ever get tired watching TV?

8. Are you listening me?

Part 3

Complete the questions with the expressions on page 95. Then ask a classmate the questions. Part of the expression may already be in the sentence.

1. What kind of music do you like to _____?

2. What time do you _____ on weekdays? On weekends?

3. Can you _____ your homework when the television is on?
   How about when the radio is on?

4. Do you like to _____ with your friends or family?

B Complete the sentences with words or phrases from the box.

access	personal	realize	solution	system
connection	public	search for	support	work

1. This beach is private. It is closed to the _____.

2. I'm going to go online to _____ that information.

3. I can't hear you very well on this cell phone. It's a poor

   _____.

4. It is important to _____ friends when they
   have problems.

5. I have been thinking about your problem and I think that I have
   a(n) _____.

6. It's not a good idea to take a lot of _____ phone calls at
   work. You should wait until you get home to talk to your friends.

7. The train _____ is very good in England. You can go
   almost anywhere in the country.

8. My cell phone doesn't _____ on the subway.

9. Not all people _____ the importance of the Internet.

10. Your company doesn't have _____ to your medical
    records. Medical information is private.

C ▸ Match the word to the word or phrase with a similar meaning.

_____	1. support	**a.** answer
_____	2. developed	**b.** private
_____	3. access	**c.** link
_____	4. search	**d.** get to
_____	5. dangerous	**e.** locate
_____	6. solution	**f.** help
_____	7. personal	**g.** look for
_____	8. communicate	**h.** able to harm you
_____	9. connection	**i.** talk
_____	10. find	**j.** created

Chapter 6 At the Movies

1. _____

2. _____

3. _____

| an action film | a drama | a musical | a romantic comedy |
| a comedy | a horror film | a mystery | |

A FIRST LOOK

A BACKGROUND BUILDING

Answer the questions below. Then share your answers with a classmate.

1. Look at the pictures on page 100. What kinds of movies do you see?
   Write the type of movie from the box on the line below the picture.

2. How often do you go to the movies? Check (✓) your answer.

   _____ once a week

   _____ once a month

   _____ twice a year

   _____ once a year

   _____ I never go to the movies.

3. Give one example for each type of movie in the box on page 100. Write
   sentences on a separate piece of paper.

   EXAMPLE: *When Harry Met Sally* is a romantic comedy.

4. What kinds of movies, or films do you like? Write *1* next to your favorite,
   2 next to your second choice, and so on.

   _____ comedies

   _____ romantic comedies

   _____ dramas

   _____ mysteries

   _____ musicals

   _____ action films

   _____ horror films

5. Work with a partner. Think about the last movie you saw and describe it to your partner. Complete the sentences.

I saw _____ last _____.
                     (title)   (week/month/year)

It is a _____ about
                (comedy/drama/mystery/other)

_____.

It was _____. I think you _____.
          (great/good/OK/terrible)   (should/shouldn't)

see it.

B READING

A Brief History of the Movies

1   Movies are "big business" all around the world. In the United States, they are big business, too. Movies have another important role; they tell us things about a country's culture.

2   Where were the first movies made? It is hard to say exactly. In the late nineteenth century, several inventors were working 5 on making movies: Thomas Edison in the United States and the Lumiere brothers in France. They called movies "moving pictures." After all, movies are actually pictures that move. The earliest whole film we have is *Fred Ott's Sneeze,* a film shot in 1891 by Edison's team. 10

3   In 1895, the Lumiere brothers opened the first "movie theater" in the world. It was in the basement of the Grand Cafe in Paris. One of the films they showed was about a train. When the audience saw the train coming toward them on the screen, they began to run away and hide. A new world was here—the 15 world of cinema.

4   Movies became very popular in the first part of the twentieth century. There were early films like *Birth of a Nation*. There were comic actors like Charlie Chaplin and actresses who played serious roles like Theda Bara. Soon, inventors no 20 longer controlled the movies. As movies started to make money, businessmen took over. Movies became an industry.

5   The next big change was the addition of sound. It is hard to believe that the only movies for over thirty years were the "silents." But in 1927 *The Jazz Singer*, the first "talkie," was 25 released. The era of silent films was over.

6   Over the years, movies have been important as entertainment. They have also painted a picture of the values and customs of different societies. A movie can show us the history of the nation it was made in, and it often reflects that 30 nation's values as well.

C TOPIC

Read the topics below. Match each topic to a paragraph in the reading. Write the number of the paragraph on the line.

_____ the first movie with sound

_____ the first movies

_____ ways that movies are important

_____ the first movie theater

_____ movies as business and culture

_____ the beginning of the movie industry

Part 1

Scan the reading for the word in column A. Write the number of the line where you find the word. Then compare the word in column A to the word in column B. Are the meanings similar or different? Write **S** (similar) or **D** (different) on the line.

	A	Line Number	B	S or D?
1.	big business		money-making	
2.	important		small	
3.	era		place	
4.	several		few	
5.	inventors		makers	
6.	team		group	
7.	audience		actors	
8.	comic		funny	
9.	controlled		managed	
10.	silents		talkies	
11.	entertainment		a source of fun	
12.	painted a picture		showed	

Part 2

Complete the sentences with words from the box.

audience	exactly	hide	screen	theater
basement	films	inventor	several	train

1. I can't tell you _____ when she was born, but it was definitely in the nineteenth century.

2. The first _____ were made before the twentieth century.

3. What time does the next _____ arrive?

4. I like to go to the movies to watch films on the big _____.

5. The _____ is below the first floor.

6. There are _____ people from France in the class.

7. That's a beautiful, old movie _____. It was built in the 1940s.

8. The children were playing a game. They ran away and found a place to _____.

9. Alexander Graham Bell was the _____ of the telephone.

10. The _____ really enjoyed her singing. They wouldn't let her leave the stage.

E ▸ READING COMPREHENSION

Circle the letter of the word or phrase that best completes each sentence.

1. Movies are big business, but they also _____ our culture.
   a. work on   **b.** believe   **c.** show

2. Movies were first invented in _____ different places.
   a. two   **b.** many   **c.** nineteen

3. Edison and the Lumieres were _____.
   a. businessmen   **b.** inventors   **c.** brothers

4. The first movies were made in the _____ century.
   a. eighteenth   **b.** twentieth   **c.** nineteenth

5. The audience in the Paris theater ran away because the train _____.
   a. wasn't real   **b.** seemed real   **c.** was late

6. _____ is an example of a comic actor.
   a. *The Jazz Singer*   **b.** Theda Bara   **c.** Charlie Chaplin

7. Talkies came _____ the silents.
   a. after   **b.** before   **c.** at the same time as

8. For over thirty years, movies were _____.
   a. big business   **b.** silent   **c.** the twentieth century

9. *Birth of a Nation* was _____ film.
   a. an early   **b.** the earliest   **c.** a talking

10. In the last paragraph, the author suggests that movies give us entertainment, show our history, and _____.
    a. paint pictures   **b.** reflect values   **c.** show the century

LOOK AGAIN

A VOCABULARY

Circle the letter of the word that best completes each sentence.

1. It was very quiet at the lake. There wasn't a(n) _____.
   a. silence   b. addition   c. sound

2. In my office, we work together. We are a _____.
   a. business   b. world   c. team

3. As soon as dinner was _____, we turned on the television.
   a. released   b. over   c. early

4. Can we change seats? I can't see the _____.
   a. role   b. audience   c. screen

5. That actress never plays a serious _____; she always does comedy.
   a. role   b. inventor   c. custom

6. The film *The Last Emperor* was _____ in Beijing.
   a. refused   b. shot   c. invented

7. They _____ a new store in the mall.
   a. realized   b. showed   c. opened

8. It's _____ to believe that you don't know who Charlie Chaplin was.
   a. hard   b. natural   c. old-fashioned

9. On weekends, people like to go to the movies for _____.
   a. big business   b. entertainment   c. money

10. People enjoy watching movies all over the _____.
    a. nation   b. world   c. era

B READING COMPREHENSION

Put the statements in order according to the reading. Number them from 1 to 6.

_____ The first movie theater opened.

_____ The earliest whole film was shot.

_____ The talkies were invented.

_____ Movies became big business.

_____ The first moving pictures were made.

_____ Silent films became popular.

C READING FOR SPECIFIC INFORMATION

The chart below lists the top ten money-making movies in the United States. Read the chart and answer the questions on page 109.

Rank	Movie Title	Year of Release	Money Made (in Millions of U.S. Dollars[*])
1.	Gone With the Wind	1939	1,188
2.	Star Wars	1977	1,027
3.	The Sound of Music	1965	824
4.	E.T.: The Extraterrestrial	1982	815
5.	The Ten Commandments	1956	758
6.	Titanic	1997	747
7.	Jaws	1975	741
8.	Doctor Zhivago	1965	701
9.	The Jungle Book	1967	627
10.	Snow White and the Seven Dwarfs	1937	615

[*]These figures were changed to reflect the value of the dollar over time.
Source: http://www.boxofficemojo.com/alltime/adjusted

1. What movie made the most money? _____

2. What is the title of the earliest movie? _____

3. What is the most recent movie? _____

4. Which of the movies do you recognize? _____

5. Which of these movies have you seen? _____

6. Why do you think that these movies made so much money? _____

_____

D▸ THINK ABOUT IT

Read the passage. Then discuss the questions with a partner.

Movie Ratings

Movies represent a culture, but what part of a culture? Some movies are made for children and some are made for adults. Movies in the United States use a rating system to show the difference. Parents began this system in 1968 to help show which films were appropriate for children. Movies for children are rated G. Movies for older children are rated PG, and movies for teenagers are rated PG-13. Teenagers must be with a parent to go to a movie rated R. Movies rated NC-17 are for adults only.

Filmmakers do not have to ask the committee for a rating. It is voluntary, but the system helps every movie find the right audience.

1. When did the rating system begin?

2. Why was it started?

3. Which movies are appropriate for teenagers?

4. What rating would you give to *Snow White and the Seven Dwarfs*?

A BACKGROUND BUILDING

Answer these questions about the picture.

1. Who is in the picture?

2. What do you think each person is thinking? How do they feel?

3. Which movie do you think the family will go to see? Why?

Read the passage. Then read the sentences on page 112. Write **T** (true), **F** (false), or **?** (not sure). You have four minutes.

My wife and kids say that I am too conservative, but I don't care. I don't think that the government should allow films that are violent, or have foul language or inappropriate sex. They should ban these movies because these movies are the reason that crime has increased. Young people watch these kinds of movies and then decide that they can do whatever they see on the screen.

Where are the old-fashioned movies where the boy meets the girl and they get married, or the cowboy fights nature by leading his cattle across a desert to reach water and grass? How about the Charlie Chaplin films? Now, those were good, entertaining movies.

I don't want to see explosions or crimes on the screen. Some psychologists say that with all the violence on TV and in movies, people are beginning not to notice it. Why not film the beauty of nature, the lives of famous inventors, or even stories about animals?

Well, what should we do? I think that the business leaders of the movie industry understand only one message: small audiences. If people refuse to go to movies, then the moviemakers will pay attention. We need to stop going and send moviemakers a message: We want them to make good movies that are appropriate for the whole family. When they see small audiences for violent films, they will stop making them.

Let's make it so that all movies have a G rating and parents don't have to be worried about what their children might see on the screen.

_____ 1. The writer is a father.

_____ 2. His wife thinks he has old-fashioned ideas.

_____ 3. The writer believes that violent movies are the cause of increased crime.

_____ 4. The writer doesn't give examples of the types of movies he thinks are acceptable.

_____ 5. The writer thinks many people don't notice violence in movies anymore.

_____ 6. The writer's solution to this problem is for the public not to go to these movies.

_____ 7. He wants violent movies to be for adults only.

_____ 8. The writer only goes to movies made for children.

_____ 9. The writer wants some movies for adults and some for children.

_____ 10. The writer wants all movies to have the same rating.

C ▸ VOCABULARY

Circle the letter of the word or phrase closest in meaning to the boldfaced word(s) in the sentence.

1. He has **conservative** ideas about the role of women.
   a. old-fashioned   **b.** natural   **c.** average

2. It's **inappropriate** to talk when someone else is talking.
   a. not right   **b.** not normal   **c.** not safe

3. A child who uses **foul** language should be punished.
   a. hard   **b.** bad   **c.** poor

4. Her father won't **allow** her to go to the dance.
   a. manage   **b.** prefer   **c.** permit

5. I'm too busy. That's the **reason** why I can't go.

   a. purpose   **b.** situation   **c.** explanation

6. Gandhi was a man who was **not violent**.

   a. peaceful   **b.** conservative   **c.** stubborn

7. His **message** was clear. He wouldn't come.

   a. question   **b.** schedule   **c.** communication

8. Did you **notice** the police car on the corner? I wonder what happened.

   a. look over   **b.** see   **c.** find

9. That movie was very **entertaining**.

   a. relaxing   **b.** special   **c.** enjoyable

10. I **refuse to** get up early. I'm on vacation.

   a. would prefer to **b.** will not   **c.** will finish

D REACT

Answer the questions. Then discuss your answers with a classmate.

1. Do you use the rating system to decide on what movies to see?

2. Have you ever not been allowed into a movie because of the rating?

3. Do you think that all movies should be G-rated for the whole family? Explain.

VOCABULARY REVIEW

A Here are words from this chapter that form expressions.

VERBS	OTHER EXPRESSIONS
be over	appropriate for
make (a movie/video)	in (1997/the past/future)
make money	once/twice/three times (a week)
refuse to (do something)	
take over	
work on	

Part 1

Complete the sentences with expressions from the box. Part of the expression may already be in the sentence.

1. Studios want to be sure that they can _____ before they decide to produce a movie.

2. Let's get together today. What time will your class _____?

3. When did Walt Disney _____ *Snow White and the Seven Dwarfs*?

4. That movie has a PG-13 rating. It's not _____ young children.

5. He goes to the movies _____.

6. The public can control the kinds of movies that are made _____ the future. They have to stop going to certain movies.

7. I'm sorry, but I can't go with you today. I have to _____ some projects at home.

8. The course meets _____: Mondays, Wednesdays, and Fridays.

9. If there is a national problem, the government will _____ the communication system.

10. I want to see that new romantic comedy, but I know my husband will _____ to see it.

Part 2

The following sentences are not correct. Add the words from the box to the sentences to make them correct. There may be more than one possible answer.

| for | in | on | once | over | to |

1. They are working their class project.

2. Is that book appropriate children?

3. He almost never goes to the movies—maybe a year.

4. I'll be finished with my work a few minutes.

5. As soon as the party was, we went to bed.

6. They made films the nineteenth century.

7. There will probably be a rating system for television the next few years.

8. She took the company in 1999, and she made it very successful.

9. They get together every Saturday—a week.

10. My teenaged sons refused go to that movie.

Part 3

Use the expressions from the box on page 114 to complete the questions. You may have to change the form of the verb. Then ask a classmate the questions.

1. Do you celebrate when a difficult course or project _____?

2. Do you think that violence in movies is _____ all audiences? Explain.

3. Did you ever _____ in an emergency situation?

4. Do you ever _____ videos?

5. Are there any movies that you _____ go see?

B **Circle the letter of the word or phrase that best completes each sentence.**

1. They are a popular group. They always have a big _____ at their concerts.
   a. public   **b.** addition   **c.** audience

2. He's a great soccer player. He's on the city _____.
   a. screen   **b.** step   **c.** team

3. Good teachers know how to _____ a large group of students.
   a. improve   **b.** locate   **c.** control

4. They _____ that film in 1995.
   a. dealt with   **b.** released   **c.** compared

5. He's a really funny actor. His movies are _____.
   a. mysteries   **b.** comedies   **c.** romances

6. Who _____ the first television?

    a. managed   **b.** invented   **c.** released

7. The movie started at _____ 7:30.

    a. exactly   **b.** later   **c.** first

8. While some movies show the history of a country, they also provide _____.

    a. addition   **b.** entertainment   **c.** situation

9. Parents want movies to teach children good _____.

    a. control   **b.** work   **c.** values

10. You should show your good points and _____ the bad.

    a. identify   **b.** reflect   **c.** hide

C   **Match each word to the word or phrase with a similar meaning.**

_____	1. business	**a.** sound
_____	2. entertainment	**b.** period of time
_____	3. invent	**c.** viewers
_____	4. era	**d.** industry
_____	5. refuse	**e.** earliest
_____	6. appropriate	**f.** fun
_____	7. noise	**g.** people who work together
_____	8. team	**h.** say no
_____	9. first	**i.** make
_____	10. audience	**j.** right

Chapter 7
Looking at Education

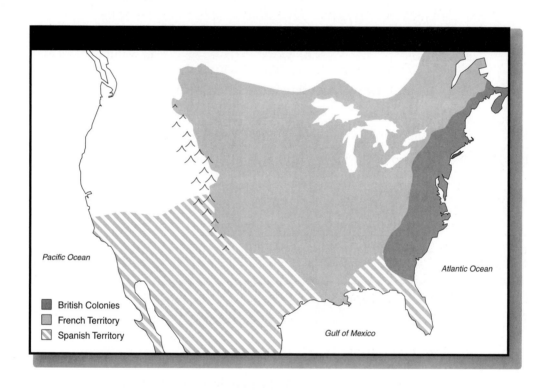

British Colonies
French Territory
Spanish Territory

Pacific Ocean

Atlantic Ocean

Gulf of Mexico

A FIRST LOOK

A BACKGROUND BUILDING

1. The map on page 118 shows the land owned by European countries in what is now the United States. Use the map to answer the questions.

   a. Can you guess what year, or what time in American history this map shows?

   b. What country controlled the most land in what is now the United States?

   c. What country had colonies on the east coast?

2. Read the chart below. Then answer the questions.

High School Students in the United States	
In public schools	89%
In private schools	11%
High School Seniors in the United States	
Who spend less than five hours a week on homework	50%
Who have a part-time job	75%

   a. Did you go to a public or a private high school?

   b. How much time did you spend on homework each week?

   c. Did you work while you were in high school?

   d. Do you think that the numbers in the chart are similar in countries other than the United States?

The History of Schools in the United States

1   The United States does not have a national school system. Each city and county has its own school system. This reflects the history of education in the United States.

2   In the early colonial days, the east coast of America was divided into three parts. The southern colonies were around   5 Virginia. The middle colonies were around New York. The New England colonies were in the Northeast.

3   The southern colonies had large farms to grow cotton. The distance between farms was very large. Education was the responsibility of each family. In the middle colonies, the people 10 came from many different countries and religious backgrounds. They set up many different schools and often taught in the language of the families: English, German, Dutch, or French. In New England, the colonists were mainly Puritans, a religious group. They lived close to each other and shared the same   15 values. They agreed on a common public school system.

4   In New England, a 1642 law said that parents had to teach their children to read. Children needed to learn about religion and the laws of the new land. Schools taught reading, writing, arithmetic, and religion (the "4 R's"). In 1647, a law said that   20 every town with fifty families had to hire a teacher.

5   There were three types of schools in New England. "Dame schools" were for the youngest children and were often in someone's house. Here children learned the alphabet and numbers. In "town schools" children learned to read, write,   25 and do arithmetic. "Latin schools" were for older boys from wealthy families. These boys learned classical languages and grammar. They often went on to the first colonial college, Harvard. Harvard was started in 1636.

6   In time, across the country, the common school became 30 normal for all children in grades 1 through 8. Taxes paid for the school, so it was free to all students. In areas with a lot of people, the children in each grade were in different classrooms. In areas with fewer people, the one-room schoolhouse was common.

7   In the 1800s, public high schools became more common. 35 They were also free and trained young people for jobs. In 1872, an important court case in Michigan said that taxes could also be used for high schools. After that, high schools were built around the country. By 1900 about 10 percent of children went to high schools. In 1930 more than 50 percent attended. By 1960, 40 it was nearly 90 percent. Today, attendance is still about 90 percent.

8   Recently, many parents have started homeschooling, or teaching their children at home. Some want their children to have more religion in their studies. Others don't think their children can get a good education in the public schools. It's interesting 45 that so many families are returning to this early form of education.

C TOPIC

Read the topics below. Match each topic to a paragraph in the reading. Write the number of the paragraph on the line.

_____ schools in New England

_____ high schools

_____ early colonial days

_____ homeschooling

_____ no national school system

_____ school for grades 1 through 8

_____ education in different areas of early America

_____ laws about education in New England

Part 1

Scan the reading for the each word in column A. Write the number of the line where you find the word. Then compare the word in column A to the word in column B. Is its meaning similar or different? Write **S** (similar) or **D** (different) on the line.

	A	Line Number	B	S or D?
1.	national		country-wide	
2.	reflects		shows	
3.	divided		put together	
4.	colonies		countries	
5.	set up		started	
6.	public		private	
7.	wealthy		rich	
8.	free		expensive	
9.	trained		prepared	
10.	court		legal	
11.	attended		went to	
12.	recently		a long time ago	

Part 2

Complete the sentences with words or phrases from the box.

attend	court	free	recently	trains
colonies	divided	national	set up	wealthy

1. We had so many students in our class that they _____ it into two sections.

2. England had _____ along what is now the east coast of the United States.

3. Many countries have a _____ education system. This means that students in different parts of the country get the same kind of education.

4. The Aviation School _____ people to fly airplanes.

5. The school doesn't cost anything. It's _____.

6. They have a lot of money. They're _____.

7. They _____ a Spanish class three times a week.

8. It didn't happen a long time ago. It happened _____.

9. I don't know how to _____ the computer. Where are the instructions?

10. A _____ case in 1872 said that taxes could be used to pay for high schools.

E ▸ READING COMPREHENSION

Circle the letter of the word or phrase that best completes each sentence.

1. There _____ a national system of education in the U.S.

   a. is   **b.** is not   **c.** may be

2. Part of what is now the U.S. was once _____.

   a. a group of colonies   **b.** a different country   **c.** in England

3. In the south, the people lived _____ each other.

   a. around   **b.** near   **c.** far away from

4. There _____ a school system in the south.

   a. was   **b.** wasn't   **c.** may be

5. A school that taught children in Dutch was probably in _____.

   a. New England   **b.** New York   **c.** the south

6. The first school system did not start in _____.

   a. the south   **b.** New England   **c.** the middle colonies

7. _____ parents in New England had to teach their children.

   a. For eighteen years,   **b.** At first,   **c.** In 1647,

8. In New England, a young child probably went to a _____.

   a. Latin school   **b.** town school   **c.** dame school

9. The first public high schools taught young people _____.

   a. the "4 R's"   **b.** Latin   **c.** job skills

10. The writer gave _____ reasons for homeschooling.

   a. one   **b.** two   **c.** three

LOOK AGAIN

A VOCABULARY

Circle the letter of the word or phrase that best completes each sentence.

1. A **colony** is a place _____.

   a. with its own government
   b. in a large country
   c. controlled by another country

2. In paragraph 3 of the reading, **public** probably means _____.

   a. open
   b. for everyone
   c. expensive

3. In paragraph 3 of the reading, **distance** describes _____.

   a. time
   b. space
   c. people

4. A **common** room is probably a room that _____.

   a. is not very nice
   b. is for one person
   c. everyone can use

5. If there is **no system**, everyone is doing something _____.

   a. wrong
   b. different
   c. good

6. In the last line of paragraph 8, **form** means _____.

   a. paper
   b. type
   c. application

7. I don't **share** a room. I _____.

   a. don't have my own room
   b. have my own room
   c. don't need my own room

8. The school was **free** for all students. The students _____.

   a. didn't have to pay any money
   b. had to pay a lot of money
   c. went to private school

9. An example of a **classical** language is _____.

   a. French
   b. English
   c. Latin

10. If you **hire** someone, you give that person _____.

    a. a job
    b. your time
    c. both a and b

An outline can help you remember important information in a reading. Complete the outline with information from "The History of Schools in the United States."

	History of Schools in the U.S.
○	
	A. Not a national system
	B. Three areas of colonies on the east coast
	1. _____
	2. _____
	3. _____
	C. Education in these areas
	1. _____
	2. _____
	3. _____
○	D. Early laws about education in New England
	1. _____
	2. _____
	E. Types of schools in New England
	1. _____
	2. _____
	3. _____
	F. The common school _____
	G. _____ became common in the 1800s
	H. _____ more popular recently
○	

C READING FOR SPECIFIC INFORMATION

Answer the question before you read the information about homeschooling.

- Do you think that homeschooling is a good idea or a bad idea? Explain why.

1   The U.S. Department of Education thinks that at least 850,000 children are homeschooled. A good education is the first reason parents want to homeschool their children. The second reason, for about 75 percent of these families, is religion. They want their children to have a religious education. They probably also don't approve of the values that children learn in regular schools.

2   Homeschoolers get their materials from many different places: libraries, bookstores, and, recently, from the Internet. Homeschooled children do as well on tests as 85 percent of children in other schools. Although parents are involved with almost all of their children's activities, homeschooled children get together with other homeschoolers to share knowledge, go on field trips, and play sports.

3   Some people don't agree with homeschooling. They say that homeschooled children don't experience the most important part of school—socializing with other children. They don't learn to be independent from their family because they are only learning their parents' point of view.

Look at the reading again. What is the topic of each paragraph? Write the topic next to its paragraph number.

Paragraph 1: _____

Paragraph 2: _____

Paragraph 3: _____

D ▶ THINK ABOUT IT

Answer the questions. Then discuss your answers with a classmate.

1. According to the passage, why are 850,000 children homeschooled?

2. What new information about homeschooling did you learn in the reading?

3. Do you think that homeschooling would be a good idea for your own children?

A BACKGROUND BUILDING

Look at the picture and discuss the questions.

1. Where are the children in this illustration?

2. Why do you think they are holding hands?

Read the passage. Then read the sentences. Write T (true), F (false), or ? (not sure). You have four minutes.

Everyone knows about the Olympics. Athletes from all over the world try to win a medal. I recently heard a story about Special Olympics. Special Olympics is for children and adults who have mental disabilities.

At a Special Olympics competition in Seattle, nine young athletes were competing in a race. The race began. The children started running, but one boy fell and started to cry. The other children heard him. They slowed down and looked back. Then, slowly, they all turned around and went back to help him stand up. The children all held hands and walked across the finish line together. The people in the audience all stood up and cheered.

Why can't we teach everyone to cooperate this way? We teach children to compete with each other, not to cooperate, but cooperation is a much more important life skill.

_____ 1. Special Olympics is the same as the Olympics.

_____ 2. The writer is an athlete.

_____ 3. In this story, one person won the race.

_____ 4. The writer saw this race on TV.

_____ 5. The athletes in this race were children.

_____ 6. The writer thinks we shouldn't have Special Olympics.

_____ 7. This story shows how important competition is.

_____ 8. All types of people compete in Special Olympics.

_____ 9. Special Olympics is for athletes with mental disabilities.

_____ 10. The racers stopped to help the person who fell.

C VOCABULARY

Circle the letter of the word or phrase closest in meaning to the boldfaced word(s) in the sentence.

1. They **compete** against a different team every Saturday.
   - **a.** meet to talk
   - **b.** play and try to win
   - **c.** practice a sport

2. This happened **recently**. I think it was last week.
   - **a.** not long ago
   - **b.** last year
   - **c.** a long time ago

3. The **race** ended in a tie. No one won.
   - **a.** competition
   - **b.** game
   - **c.** club

4. The first runner crossed the **finish** line in three hours and two minutes.
   - **a.** running
   - **b.** race
   - **c.** end

5. I played soccer in high school, but I wasn't a very good **athlete**.
   - **a.** sports player
   - **b.** competitor
   - **c.** student

6. The **cheers** from the audience lasted for five minutes.
   - **a.** yells of support
   - **b.** noise
   - **c.** clapping

7. If you **cooperate**, you will find a solution to the problem quickly.
   - **a.** compete
   - **b.** discuss
   - **c.** work together

8. What **skills** do you need to fly a plane? Does it take a long time to learn?
   - **a.** practice
   - **b.** gifts
   - **c.** abilities

9. She kept the **medal** all her life. She was very proud of it.
   - **a.** clothing
   - **b.** award
   - **c.** souvenir

10. After his injury, he had a **mental** disability. He got confused easily.
    - **a.** of the body
    - **b.** of the mind
    - **c.** short-term

D REACT

Discuss the questions in a small group.

1. What was more important to the children in the reading, winning the race (competition), or helping each other (cooperation)?

2. Which do you think is harder to teach children, competition or cooperation? Why?

3. Which is better in the following situations, competition or cooperation? Check (✓) your answer.

	Competition	Cooperation
In sports		
In the family		
In math class		
At work		

VOCABULARY REVIEW

 A Here are words from this chapter that form expressions.

VERBS		
agree with (someone) about (something)	compete (with someone) in (a race/competition)	set up
		slow down
approve of	hold hands	stand up
be divided into	know (much/a lot) about (something)	turn around

Part 1

Complete the sentences with expressions from the box.

1. Young children usually _____ with their parents when they cross the street.

2. The parents and the teacher had different ideas about how to teach reading. They didn't _____ each other _____ reading.

3. You're going in the wrong direction. You need to _____ and go back.

4. Germany used to _____ East and West. Now it's one country.

5. Most people don't _____ the use of bad language in public.

6. The high school swim team is very good. They _____ other high schools _____ national competitions.

7. In many schools, when an adult enters a classroom, the children _____.

8. I asked a friend to help me _____ my new
   computer system.

9. She drives too fast. I wish she would _____.

10. I don't _____ very much _____
    American history.

Part 2

The following sentences are not correct. Add the words from the box to the sentences to make them correct. There may be more than one answer.

about	around	down	into	of	up	with

1. You're going too fast. Slow!

2. We'd better turn. I think we drove past the driveway.

3. Their team has a lot of very good players. It's hard to compete them.

4. I don't agree them about the school, but they have a right to their own
   point of view.

5. The big piece of cake was divided three pieces.

6. We're best friends, but we don't agree with each other everything.

7. Do you know anything computers? Mine is not working.

8. As soon as we moved, I called the telephone company to set my
   telephone service.

9. My parents don't approve the clothing I wear on weekends.

Part 3

Complete the questions with expressions from the list on page 132. Then ask a classmate the questions.

1. When you're driving and you see a police officer, do you
   _____?

2. Do you _____ much _____ football?

3. Do you always _____ your parents, or do you have
   different opinions?

4. Did you ever _____ a contest or other competition? If so,
   what was it?

B Complete the sentences with words from the box.

athlete	common	disabilities	hire	share
attend	compete	distance	law	wealthy

1. She likes to do sports. She's a good _____.

2. This week, some of the students will _____ in the
   science fair.

3. I _____ a public school.

4. How far is your house from the school? What's the _____
   between them?

5. Children with learning _____ may need more help from
   the teacher.

6. We need to use a dictionary in class, but we only have one. We'll have to
   _____ it.

7. Private schools are usually quite expensive, so you have to be
_____ to send your children to one.

8. The company needed more workers, so they decided to
_____ twenty people.

9. You can't smoke in elevators. There's a _____ against it.

10. The colonists agreed to have a _____ public
school system.

C Match each word to the word or phrase with a similar meaning.

_____ 1. set up   **a.** of the mind

_____ 2. race   **b.** of the body

_____ 3. train   **c.** show

_____ 4. colony   **d.** use something together

_____ 5. compete   **e.** start or get ready

_____ 6. national   **f.** try to win

_____ 7. physical   **g.** teach or learn a skill

_____ 8. share   **h.** competition

_____ 9. reflect   **i.** of the country

_____ 10. mental   **j.** a place governed by another country

Chapter 8 Smoking or Non-smoking?

A FIRST LOOK

A BACKGROUND BUILDING

Write answers to these questions. Then share your answers with a classmate.

1. Why do you think the people in the picture on page 136 are smoking outside?

2. How do you think they feel about smoking outside?

3. If you smoke, answer the following:

   a. How many packs of cigarettes do you smoke each week?

   b. Why do you smoke?

4. If you are not a smoker, why don't you smoke?

5. Do your friends or members of your family smoke?

6. Who do you think smokes more, men or women?

Why Do People Smoke?

1   Smoking is now an international habit, but it began in the Americas. Native American Indians gave Christopher Columbus a gift of tobacco in 1492. Columbus and other early explorers took tobacco back to Europe. From Europe, tobacco spread to Asia.

2   There are probably many reasons why people smoke.   5
Some just like the taste of tobacco; others enjoy the comfort that a cigarette gives. Others have gotten used to smoking. It has become a habit. For some of these people, smoking is a psychological habit. For others, smoking is a physical habit: Their bodies need the nicotine. They are addicted to smoking.   10

3   Why do teenagers start to smoke? Many young people probably enjoy smoking because it is a dangerous, adult activity. There is probably a lot of peer pressure to smoke. "All my friends are smoking. Why shouldn't I?" Also, smoking is probably considered sophisticated or "cool."   15

4   According to doctors, the biggest question about smoking is not, "Why do people smoke?" It is "How can people stop smoking?" Some people can stop "cold turkey"; that is, they decide to stop, and they do—they never pick up another cigarette. Some people cut down on cigarettes gradually; they   20
smoke one fewer each day or they change to a cigarette with less nicotine. Other people decide to stop but find that they can't. They start smoking again. They are really addicted to smoking.

5   Research on smoking and health began in the early 1900s.   25
By the 1950s, it was clear that smoking caused lung cancer.

Starting in 1965, in the United States, all cigarette packs had warnings about the dangers of smoking.

6   In 1975, Minnesota became the first state to pass laws against second-hand smoke, the smoke from other people's cigarettes. The state made an anti-smoking law for public places and public meetings. This was the first law in the United States that separated smokers and nonsmokers. Airlines and restaurants also started to have both smoking and nonsmoking sections. In 1983, San Francisco banned smoking in private workplaces. In 1987, Congress banned smoking on U.S. airline flights of less than two hours. All over the U.S. and Canada, smoke-free restaurants and workplaces became common. It became harder and harder for smokers to find a place to smoke in public in the United States and Canada. 40

7   Today, almost all airlines around the world ban smoking. Some cities ban smoking in public places, and smoke-free areas are becoming more common everywhere. Is the anti-smoking movement going international?

C TOPIC

Read the topics below. Match each topic to a paragraph in the reading. Write the number of the paragraph on the line.

_____ reasons why young people smoke

_____ reasons why people smoke

_____ smoking around the world today

_____ laws against smoking

_____ smoking and health

_____ information about the history of smoking

_____ how people stop smoking

Part 1

Scan the reading for each word in column A. Write the number of the line where you find the word. Then compare the word in column A to the word in column B. Is its meaning similar or different? Write **S** (similar) or **D** (different) on the line.

A	Line Number	B	S or D?
1. spread		moved	
2. enjoy		like	
3. psychological		physical	
4. addicted		not able to stop	
5. teenagers		adults	
6. peer pressure		approval from parents	
7. sophisticated		cool	
8. stop cold turkey		stop gradually	
9. research		study	
10. warnings		notices	
11. anti-smoking		against smoking	
12. banned		allowed	

Part 2

Complete the sentences with words or phrases from the box.

addicted	cut down	gift	international
banned	dangerous	habit	section

1. Getting enough sleep is a good _____.

2. Tomorrow is Maria's birthday, so we need to buy her a(n) _____.

3. London is a(n) _____ city. It has people from all over the world.

4. I eat too much candy. I have to _____.

5. I can't stop drinking coffee. I think I'm _____ to it.

6. This is a smoke-free restaurant. We don't have a smoking _____.

7. Cigarettes can be _____ to your health.

8. Smoking is _____ on all flights that are less than two hours.

E ▸ READING COMPREHENSION

Circle the letter of the word or phrase that best completes each sentence.

1. Smoking tobacco began in _____.
   a. Asia   **b.** Europe   **c.** the Americas

2. Tobacco went from Europe to _____.
   a. America   **b.** Asia   **c.** the world

3. According to the reading, people smoke because they like the _____ and comfort of cigarettes.
   a. habit   **b.** taste   **c.** tobacco

4. When smokers are addicted, they _____ nicotine.
   a. need   **b.** quit   **c.** both a and b

5. According to the reading, some _____ smoke because it is dangerous.
   a. people   **b.** teenagers   **c.** adults

6. The reading says that teenagers smoke because it is an adult activity, it is "cool," and because their _____ smoke.
   a. parents   **b.** brothers   **c.** friends

7. The biggest question for doctors, according to the reading is:
   a. Which people like smoking?   **b.** Why do people like smoking?   **c.** How can people stop smoking?

8. Some people quit smoking by cutting down on cigarettes gradually. Others _____ when they quit.
   a. smoke less   **b.** become addicted   **c.** stop cold turkey

9. By the 1950s, we had information about smoking and _____.
   a. smoking sections   **b.** addiction   **c.** cancer

10. Almost all airlines around the world _____ smoking.
    a. ban   **b.** allow   **c.** do not ban

LOOK AGAIN

A VOCABULARY

Circle the letter of the word or phrase that best completes each sentence.

1. At first only one person was sick, but then it _____ to others.
   a. spread   **b.** addicted   **c.** gave

2. The teachers need to _____ the two children who fight with each other.
   a. ban   **b.** start   **c.** separate

3. "Oh, come on. Everyone does it" is an example of _____.
   a. a sentence   **b.** peer pressure   **c.** psychology

4. The little girl wanted to wear _____ clothes like her older sister.
   a. physical   **b.** sophisticated   **c.** healthy

5. I'm running out of money, so I need to _____ on my expenses.
   a. cut down   **b.** start   **c.** ban

6. _____ means related to your mind.
   a. Physical   **b.** Addiction   **c.** Psychological

7. Once a year I go to the doctor for a _____ examination.
   a. physical   **b.** psychological   **c.** nicotine

8. The first time I visited Paris, I took a guided tour of the city. However, the next time I go there, I plan to _____ the city by myself.
   a. start   **b.** explore   **c.** find

9. It's hard to stop doing something that is a _____.
   a. change   **b.** reason   **c.** habit

10. _____ is in cigarette tobacco.
    a. Tobacco   **b.** Cancer   **c.** Nicotine

B ▶ READING COMPREHENSION

Answer the questions.

1. Where did tobacco come from? _____

2. Who brought tobacco to Europe? _____

3. According to the reading, what are some reasons why people smoke?

   a. _____

   b. _____

   c. _____

4. According to the reading, what are the reasons why teenagers smoke?

   a. _____

   b. _____

   c. _____

5. Some people quit smoking cold turkey. What does that mean?

   _____

6. Some smokers cut down on cigarettes. What do these smokers do?

   _____

7. Put the following information in order from 1 to 6 according to the reading.

   _____ Smoking was first banned on airplanes.

   _____ Research showed that smoking caused cancer.

   _____ Smokers have trouble finding a place to smoke.

   _____ Tobacco was used in the Americas.

   _____ Research on smoking began.

   _____ Tobacco spread from Europe to Asia.

The chart below shows the percentage of men and women over age 15 who smoke in 12 countries. Read the chart. Then answer the questions.

Percentages of Men and Women Who Smoke in Selected Countries		
Country	**Men**	**Women**
Republic of Korea	67.0	6.7
Russian Federation	67.0	30.0
China	61.0	7.0
Japan	59.0	14.8
France	40.0	27.0
Argentina	40.0	23.0
Brazil	39.9	25.4
Egypt	39.8	1.0
Mexico	38.3	14.4
Switzerland	36.0	26.0
United States	28.1	23.5
Nigeria	24.4	6.7
SOURCE: World Health Organization, 2001.		

1. Write three facts from the chart.

EXAMPLE: A higher percentage of women smoke in Switzerland than in Egypt.

Fact 1: ─────────────────────────────

Fact 2: ─────────────────────────────

Fact 3: ─────────────────────────────

2. Look at rates of smoking for women. Which countries have a similar percentage of women who smoke?

3. Which countries have similar rates of smoking among men?

4. In which country is the difference between the percentages of male and female smokers greatest?

5. In which country is the difference between the percentages of male and female smokers smallest?

D THINK ABOUT IT

Check (✓) the statements you agree with. Then discuss your choices with a partner.

_____ I will tell my children not to smoke.

_____ I will tell my children to smoke if they want to.

_____ In my opinion, smoking in workplaces is OK.

_____ In my opinion, smoking in workplaces is not OK.

_____ In my opinion, smoking in restaurants is OK.

_____ In my opinion, smoking in restaurants is not OK.

_____ It's fine with me if people smoke in my house or apartment.

_____ The government should make rules about smoking in public places.

_____ Each restaurant or bar should have its own rules about smoking.

A BACKGROUND BUILDING

Answer these questions about the picture.

1. Match the following with the labels in the picture.

———— judge

———— jury

———— defense lawyer

———— plaintiffs

2. What do you think this court case might be about?

Read the passage. Then read the sentences. Write T (true), F (false), or ? (not sure). You have four minutes.

Who Is Responsible?

I'm on a jury in a court in Florida. The plaintiffs are the family of a man who died from lung cancer. They are suing the cigarette manufacturer. The family says that the company is responsible. It is a difficult case. Who is responsible when someone dies from lung cancer—the smoker or the cigarette manufacturer?

Did you know that 1,200 people die every day in the United States from illnesses related to smoking? And did you know that the cigarette companies have known about the dangers of smoking since the 1960s? They knew there was a link between smoking and cancer, and they knew that nicotine was addictive.

On the other hand, the manufacturer says that the man made the choice to smoke. He could have stopped at any time, but he didn't. Other people quit smoking. The defense lawyers for the manufacturer say that the man is responsible for his choice to smoke; the company is not.

I don't really know what to think. It's terrible to die from smoking. It's terrible that the cigarette companies knew how unhealthy cigarettes were but continued to sell them. But is it their fault that he decided to smoke? That he liked it? That he kept on smoking and then couldn't stop? I don't know. This is a very difficult decision.

_____ 1. The writer is a judge.

_____ 2. The man who smoked is suing the cigarette manufacturer.

_____ 3. The man tried to stop smoking.

_____ 4. The case is against all cigarette manufacturers.

_____ 5. The man who smoked has already died.

_____ 6. Cigarette companies knew about the dangers of smoking in the 1950s.

_____ 7. 1,200 people die every year from smoking.

_____ 8. Cancer is the only illness caused by smoking.

C VOCABULARY

Part 1

Match the word to its definition.

_____ 1. **court**

_____ 2. **danger**

_____ 3. **jury**

_____ 4. **kept on**

_____ 5. **link**

_____ 6. **manufactures**

_____ 7. **quit**

_____ 8. **related**

_____ 9. **responsible for**

_____ 10. **sue**

a. continued

b. take someone to court

c. place where a judge works

d. people who listen in a courtroom and make a decision about whether someone is guilty or innocent

e. something that joins two things; connection

f. makes; produces

g. stop

h. connected

i. the cause of

j. unsafe condition or situation

Part 2

Complete the sentences with the boldfaced words from Part 1.

1. The _____ decided that the man was not guilty. They didn't think he was the murderer.

2. Are her problems with her health _____ to smoking cigarettes?

3. The company _____ clothing for children.

4. There is a clear _____ between smoking and many diseases.

5. They didn't pay their bills. We had to take them to _____.

6. Do you realize the _____ of driving so fast?

7. After I broke my leg, I decided to _____ skiing.

8. He didn't give up. He _____ trying to find the answer.

9. The man in the blue car was _____ the accident. He was driving too fast.

10. That man sold me a television that doesn't work and he won't give me back my money. I will have to _____ him.

D REACT

1. Read "Who Is Responsible?" on page 148 again. Divide the class into two groups.

    Group A: You are the defense lawyers for the cigarette company. Decide what arguments you will use in the trial.

    Group B: You are the lawyers for the smoker's family. Decide what arguments you will use in the trial.

2. Both sides present your arguments to the class.

3. Now, everyone becomes a member of the jury. What is your decision? Who is responsible—the cigarette manufacturer or the smoker?

VOCABULARY REVIEW

A Here are words from this chapter that form expressions.

VERBS	OTHER EXPRESSIONS
die from	addicted to
enjoy (doing something)	for or against
get used to	a law against
start (to do/doing something)	related to
stop (doing something)	responsible for

Part 1

Complete the sentences with expressions from the box. Part of the expression may already be in the sentence.

1. I really don't like the change in our time schedule. I can't
   _____ it.

2. Please _____ driving so fast. There's too much traffic.

3. Who is _____ the accident? That person should pay to fix
   the car.

4. When did you _____ smoking? When you were
   a teenager?

5. My wife and I _____ going out to dinner on weekends.

6. I'm going to quit smoking because I don't want to
   _____ cancer.

7. He can't stop smoking. He is _____ cigarettes.

8. Is her illness _____ her smoking?

9. Are you for or _____ my idea?

10. You can't smoke in the library. There is a _____ smoking in public buildings.

Part 2

The following sentences are not correct. Add the words from the box to the sentences to make them correct.

against	for	from	to

1. She is addicted smoking.

2. I work from 3:00 until 11:00. I can't get used this schedule.

3. He died old age, not cancer.

4. Are you or against smoking in restaurants?

5. Don't worry. You are not responsible the problem.

6. I don't have a cold. I think my sneezing is related allergies.

7. When she entered high school, she started smoke.

8. They have a law making too much noise in this town.

9. There is new research that shows red wine is related good health.

Part 3

Use the expressions on page 151 to complete the questions. Then ask a classmate the questions. Part of the expression may already be in the sentence.

1. What do you enjoy _____ on weekends?

2. What is one thing you are for and another thing you
   are _____?

3. Did you ever try to stop _____ something and have a
   hard time? If so, what was it?

4. What is one thing that was hard for you to get _____?

B **Circle the letter of the word or phrase that best completes each sentence.**

1. I had a hard time when I tried to quit _____.
   a. smoke   **b.** smoker   **c.** smoking

2. The school _____ smoking. They did not allow anyone to smoke in
   the building.
   a. sued   **b.** banned   **c.** cut down on

3. I can't quit, but I have _____ smoking.
   a. stopped   **b.** cut down on   **c.** kept on

4. People who get lung cancer often are or were smokers. Smoking and
   cancer are _____.
   a. banned   **b.** psychological   **c.** related

5. It's not my fault. I am not _____ for this problem.
   a. addicted   **b.** sophisticated   **c.** responsible

6. They took the company to court because they thought the company
   caused the problem. They _____ the company.
   a. sued   **b.** judged   **c.** linked

7. I can't stop drinking that kind of soda. I'm _____ to it.

    a. related   **b.** addicted   **c.** responsible

8. I wash my face as soon as I wake up every morning. It's a(n) _____.

    a. habit   **b.** case   **c.** addiction

9. I don't like to exercise, but I _____ doing it because I know it's important for my health.

    a. quit   **b.** cut down on   **c.** keep on

10. She was only 13 years old, but she looked like she was 18 because she wore very _____ clothes.

    a. expensive   **b.** sophisticated   **c.** physical

C Match each word or phrase to the word or phrase with a similar meaning.

_____ 1. link   **a.** someone who is at the same level

_____ 2. spread   **b.** grown up

_____ 3. habit   **c.** reduce

_____ 4. quit   **d.** study

_____ 5. sue   **e.** stop

_____ 6. cut down   **f.** not allow

_____ 7. sophisticated   **g.** something a person always does

_____ 8. peer   **h.** move to cover a larger area

_____ 9. research   **i.** take to court

_____ 10. ban   **j.** connection